New British Architecture

New British Architecture

Robert Maxwell

Thames and Hudson · London

First published in Great Britain by
Thames and Hudson Ltd, London 1972
© Verlag Gerd Hatje, Stuttgart 1972

Printed and bound in West Germany

0 500 34054 4

Contents

Preface   7

Introduction   8

Notes   31

Single-family houses   32

Multi-family houses   54

Student buildings   78

University buildings   100

Hospitals and schools   130

Sports buildings   146

Civic centres   152

Cultural and institutional buildings   158

Commercial buildings   176

Transport buildings   194

Index of architects   199

Photo credits   200

Preface

British architecture is a peculiar animal. Apparently riddled with formalism, it continues to provide a social service. The architects are used: about 75 % of all building construction is handled by them. Half of them are in salaried employment, mainly in the public service, and public institutions provide the main commissions for the rest. The land is not owned by the community, but neither is it freely exploitable by the private individual. Britain is a land of compromise in which nothing extreme is allowed to happen, either good or bad: yet it reflects enough of the contradictions of the capitalist system to reveal the problems which face the architect who wants to reform as well as to serve society.

In the sixties, modern architecture the world over entered a period of uncertain values. Ostensibly based on the ideals of objectivity, functionality and the furtherance of social good, it was in fact pressed into service by sectarian forces of all kinds. Instead of becoming universal, it became partisan. In Britain these tendencies show as clearly as elsewhere, but are softened by the widespread assumption that architecture is not in any case an art, and that buildings, whether ugly or beautiful, efficient or inefficient, are not of great importance. The greatest volume of building in Britain is carried out either by the local authorities or under the direct control of their planning departments. The hand of bureaucracy has contrived to ensure that most of this building is dull, unenterprising, innocuous in the particular, conventional in the mass. It is not often represented in this book.

What is represented here is the kind of architecture which is attempting to extend the range of convention, whether in a big way or in a small way: architects' architecture, if you like — although the selection is not confined, I hope, to a single preferred style. Necessarily, most of the examples are by private architects who have been able to negotiate some degree of freedom of expression with their clients. These architects face a problem: how much are they to allow the interests of the client to pre-empt those of the user? To whom is the building to appeal? Can it be understood by a few or by all men?

In making this selection, which I admit is arbitrary, I make no apology for dealing with the buildings in terms of their form. To establish the weight of the objective content in so many examples would be a work of delicate research in itself: the scientific study of buildings as composite systems, their generation from the programme and their performance in use, is still an infant subject. I assume that rationality, in the majority of cases, is a sufficient ingredient in the methodology to ensure that the architect's analysis is genuinely predictive, and that the buildings get used approximately as he expected. What I am interested in is the area where he has exercised freedom of choice, and the extent to which that freedom has been necessarily limited by the contract between the individual and society. Here we are up against the arbitrary nature of form, its essential two-facedness, and the role of interpretation — both that exercised by the architect in the choice of form, and that forced on the user insofar as he is susceptible to the appearance of the building during his subjection to it. I have therefore limited my discussion, in the introduction which follows, to architecture considered as an expressive system. I have also limited myself langely to the works of the sixties, avoiding the dangerous temptation to identify the theoretical trends and the future. Archigram is, for the moment, eliminated by this arbitrary classification, but not, I am glad to say, Cedric Price.

The texts attached to the examples have been drafted by me, but follow closely the factual information supplied by the architects, for whose help and collaboration I am very grateful. I am not, on the other hand, responsible for the fact that the overwhelming majority of the pictures provided are devoid of people. Why? That is certainly a good question.

To Gerd Hatje, who asked me to undertake this book, my gratitude is due for his interest — and patience.

Robert Maxwell
February 1972

7

Introduction

The English tradition: feeling and principles

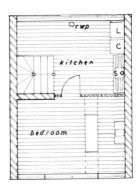

Brett: 'I take it then that the first question the critic of architecture must ask himself is this: is this serious?'
Lubetkin: 'I would even say that unless it is serious in the sense of our discussion it is hardly worth reviewing.'
Brett: 'And I suppose his second question must be this. Where does this building fit in? Is it in advance, in retreat, or just dug in waiting for something to happen?'
Lubetkin: 'Yes, that must be asked. But it will not always be easy to answer it. How can you tell the difference between advance and retreat when you are so hazy about your social and aesthetic objectives?'
Brett: 'Oh, I can't define the direction, but I know an advance when I see one.'
Lubetkin: 'How English!'[1]

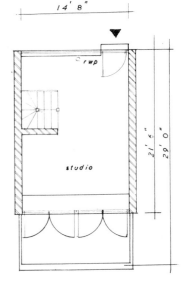

Nikolaus Pevsner once defended the English tradition of the Picturesque against the attacks of an art critic who had condemned it for its lack of seriousness, its subjectivism and its dependence on ephemeral notions of taste.[2] He defended it as a living tradition — one which applied in 1950 as much as in 1800 — on the grounds that it required and exploited a free mind, an eye for the unexpected and a sensitivity to the values of whole situations rather than to those of rule-of-thumb methods. He went so far as to claim that the Picturesque was 'the first feeling-your-way theory of art in European history and far the greatest contribution England has made to aesthetic theory'.

Pevsner saw the English tradition as according a stronger place to *feeling* than to *principles,* both of these being equally valid as stimuli to art. The English tradition would then appear to lean towards empirical values and ad-hoc solutions, a bias which is especially appropriate to the planner, since the practice of planning scarcely admits of anything more utopian.

The architect too should benefit from this more flexible approach. During the first half of the twentieth century, when the principles of the Academy and of the Beaux-Arts were no longer acceptable, 'the artist had to feel his way, explore, risk and often fail, but the architect doing the same succeeded — succeeded in reaching the safe ground of locus and usus.'[3] Safe ground presumably because for the architect limitations of situation and use combined to reduce the risk of being wild, mad or wrong.

Pevsner's analysis does not go very deeply into first causes; his method is scholarly rather than scientific, and he makes no attempt to offer an explanation as to why the architect should have arrived more readily on safe ground than the artist; nor, for that matter, under what conditions a feeling-your-way theory of art may be better than a certainty-of-truth theory of art. He could be right, however, if we are prepared to allow some degree of utilitarian value to all forms of art, if only in the general sense that the inventions of art contribute to the life-style of a culture and are an indispensable element in the development of fresh values to meet changing conditions. Seen in these terms, Pevsner's feeling-your-way theory of art adumbrates a cybernetic process, in which a goal of adaptation is achieved through a dynamic balance between feeling (a sensing device) and principles (a governing device) within constraints of situation and use which ensure reiteration and continuity.

It would be absurd to claim that British architecture as a whole demonstrates better than any other what regular process of adaptation and development may be under way. And yet there may be some advantage in looking at British architecture of the decade of the sixties in some such terms. It is not that the situation in Britain is unique: architecture is increasingly playing a part in the formation of a single world-wide culture. It is true that in Britain there has been a remarkable continuity of development of a modern vernacular. Nowhere in Britain has there been a revulsion against non-traditional forms or an undue adherence to traditional forms such as marks the reconstruction of Saint-Lô, Warsaw, or Ulm. Hating novelty as they do, the English have accepted new styles of architecture without a change of heart.

There was hardly any modern architecture in England before 1939. Since 1945 is has become the accepted style. The penalty of this smooth conversion has been that the new architecture was acceptable because it was seen as humdrum. And humdrum it usually was. The English scene is tolerant, good humoured, well-meaning, and perhaps as a consequence lacking in precision.

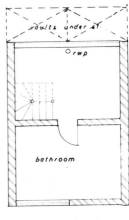

For projects the given years refer to the date of design; for executed buildings, to the beginning of construction.

1, 2. Alison & Peter Smithson. Town house in Soho Project. 1952.

2

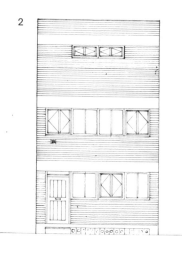

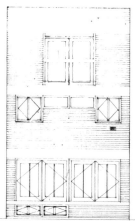

Brett: 'Unfortunately, precision is not a virtue the English admire. Character and atmosphere are the sort of words they use in praise, and the more indefinable a building's attributes, the more they like it. Of the two recognized ways of seeing, the classical tradition of formal discipline and the romantic vision of the building as sculpture, they keep veering back towards the romantic. It's the climate, of course.'[4]

It could be the climate, or the system of government, or the influence of a common law based on precedent rather than premise. Whatever the reason, British architecture appears to favour a low-key and gradualist approach, distrustful alike of formal polemics and intellectual pretensions. When Pevsner wrote his defence of the English Picturesque tradition, the pervading tone of English practice was that mixture of realism and mild sentimentality which came to be known as the New Empiricism.[5] Never was the English scene so characteristically English.

The Labour victory in the 1945 election had unexpectedly dispossessed the war hero Churchill and inaugurated an era of social justice and the common man, within limits. The English were playing at being social-democrats. In the field of architecture, the same feeling of decency and fair play was evident. C. H. Aslin's remarkable initiative at the Hertfordshire County Architect's Department had led to the development of CLASP (Consortium for Local Authorities Special Programme), and a rational building programme in schools, where for the first time the provision of buildings was treated as a coherent part of an educational service to the community. The school buildings themselves were casual and cheap, pleasant and undemanding. In housing, the predominant aim was to create variety and familiarity. When 20-storey tower blocks were employed (so as to free the ground for 'open space') they were humanized by the use of brick facings and window boxes, Swedish style. In the field of planning, the government was committed to a policy of reducing the inhuman pressures of London by the creation of a green belt with an outer ring of satellite towns to take the 'overspill' — a policy based on Patrick Abercrombie's ideas and his Plan for Greater London, itself derived from the garden city tradition of Ebenezer Howard. All of these developments, however, were diffuse and incoherent. It would have been difficult for Pevsner to see this scene as an authentic part of the English Picturesque tradition had it not been for the special concentration of these characteristics which had crystallized in the South Bank Exhibition of the Festival of Britain in 1951.

The South Bank Exhibition was intended to be a boost to morale and production in the midst of post-war scarcities, and a promise of better things to come. It was intended at the architectural level to demonstrate that a vernacular of modern architecture already existed. The common man had been inclined to identify modern architecture as flat-roofed and peculiar: the pavilions on the South Bank were to show him that it had a human face. Britain was still great, of course, but a purely technological gesture comparable to Paxton's incredible demonstration of industrial prefabrication in the Great Exhibition of 1851 would have been entirely out of place.

Instead, Hugh Casson coordinated with ingenuity and tact a deliberate scatter of small-scale pavilions around Basil Spence's Dome of Discovery, linked loosely though landscape and townscape, making up a total environment in which nothing was excessively imposed and yet nothing was altogether accidental.

It is not so surprising that this demonstration of the 'carefully careless'[6] by his friends should have convinced Pevsner that the English Picturesque tradition was alive and well. Other members of *The Architectural Review* team, however, such as Gordon Cullen and Ian Nairn, proselytized for the Picturesque with a zeal which suggested despair rather than hope. In the country at large, Picturesque values where they were already in existence, in country houses, villages and the old centres of towns, seemed to be doomed to erosion from the twin pressures of development and the automobile.

To the younger generation of architects — those whose contributions to British architecture would not be realized until the sixties — the style of the Festival of Britain seemed at best sentimental, at worst, effete. It lacked seriousness. It was bland, and it was parochial. Modern architecture had been sold short in Britain.

The sixties were to be immensely successful for two top architects already well established in the profession — Sir Basil Spence, the doyen of the establishment, and Richard Seifert, the darling of the developers. Both were able to operate in a climate of great permissiveness. The myth of functionalism and the puritan belief in utilitarianism which had hitherto dominated the modern movement were due to give way to a decade of formalism. This phenomenon was to declare itself at a world scale. Its origins may not be traceable to any single country or architect. The work of Johnson in the United

States, of Niemeyer in Brazil, of Moretti in Italy, of the Metabolists in Japan, of a dozen western architects working in the capitals of oil sheikdoms or developing republics, all contributed their part. Not least important was the crucial moment when Le Corbusier went soft with Ronchamp. The sixties were to be the decade of Brutalism, and Britain was to contribute an essential ingredient in the intellectual dismemberment of the rationalist ethic.

3

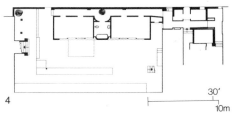

4

Brutalism: the intensification of feeling and principles

Pevsner's assessment of the English Picturesque tradition as being alive and well seems in retrospect to have been rather optimistic. The erosion of the visual environment has proceeded apace since he wrote (in 1954). But it is not merely the accumulating loss of visual amenity which has led to a revival, in the seventies, of the forces of conservatism. A deeper crisis is apparent today, and on a world scale. This crisis is involved with ethics as much as with aesthetics; it is expressed largely through the attitudes of the younger generation disillusioned with material progress and the immobility of institutions. The polarity between the life-styles of the younger generation and the rest of society is today everywhere evident.

In 1954, however, this polarity was only beginning to emerge. It says something for the virtues of the easy-going English tradition that the revolt could happen in architecture as early as in other fields. (In France the situation in architecture continued to worsen throughout the sixties until the events of May 1968.) But it was precisely the easy-going and humdrum characteristics which were seized on as objectionable, whether they constituted a genuine Picturesque tradition or not. The system was condemned as being out of touch with reality – economic reality as much as anything – but above all it was estranged from the fundamental trends in society, the pressures behind mere appearance. And equally it was out of touch with ideas: it dealt in banalities and accepted values, and could not therefore face the real problems or inject fresh values into the scene for fear of upsetting the balance of the picture.

This point of view was put with the greatest weight by Alison and Peter Smithson, since for the first time in living memory they offered at the same time a new ideological position expressed in words, and projects, even buildings, which illustrated it:

'It is necessary to create an architecture of reality.

An architecture which takes as its starting point the period 1910 – of de Stijl, Dada and Cubism – and which ignores the waste land of the four functions.

An art *concerned with the natural order,* the poetic relationship between living things and environment.

We wish to see towns and buildings which do not make us feel ashamed, ashamed that we cannot realise the potential of the twentieth century, ashamed that philosophers and physicists must think us fools, and painters think us irrelevant.

We live in moron-made cities.

Our generation must try and produce evidence that men are at work.'[7]

The Smithsons' 'invention' of Brutalism has been well documented by Reyner Banham.[8] It is most frequently illustrated by their secondary school at Hunstanton in Norfolk, which was the first building in the canon of Brutalism to be constructed, and 'which immediately achieved international recognition. Yet in some ways this is a pity, for this design has attracted a certain popular discussion which has tended to obscure the philosophical issues raised. Its physical properties were impugned – bare brickwork is unsympathetic to noisy children; and its metaphysical properties were attacked – its vocabulary is Miesian and appears both derivative and high church in the context of a school-building programme. Indeed the building, which was intended as architecture, has been judged rather as a school, while ignoring the interest of the planning principle it adopted through which staircases are substituted for corridors and horizontal circulation removed from the upper level.

A design which is unbuilt though not unpublished, and which has attracted little notice, may better illustrate through its utter simplicity the nature of the issues which were at stake: this is the Smithsons' project for a town house in Soho (ill. 1,2) for their own occupation. Their first years in London had been spent in a little Georgian house in Doughty Street, and the virtues of living in the city centre, and of exploiting the vertical space envelope created by the existing fabric of party walls, was very much in mind. Here no issues of social context and reaction have arisen to spoil the significance of

5

10

6

their action. And the meaning is clear: the architects wanted to push away all false sentiment and reveal the poetry in the natural order. Bare brickwork and a carpenter's winding wooden stair are arranged to create the maximum of intelligibility from the simplest of elements. As at Hunstanton, utility and luxury are bedfellows here. The space envelope is a little tower and energetic use of the staircase is assumed to be self-evident. The different character of each floor within the same boundary walls is what makes both the utility and the poetry of the house. Thus the only bathroom is in the basement, but it is the whole width of the house. The living-room occupies the top storey, where the completed staircase will not interrupt the largest possible spread of space. It is not only the raw surfaces, but the disposition of functions and spaces, which achieves economy and expresses a direct approach to fundamentals. This is, and is meant to be, truth to reality, to life, at a basic level.

At the same time, considered purely as form, the building is an interesting statement. Its raw qualities are expressed on the outside as alternate bands of brick and concrete, which convey the character of a small warehouse.[9] It may be interpreted as a rude gesture towards the polite Georgian tradition, or even as an anti-art gesture of a Dadaist kind (in line with the Smithsons' primitive hut with its suggestions of survival and holocaust, in the 'This is tomorrow' exhibition of 1956). While this rudeness is undoubtedly there, we may notice on the other hand that the disposition of the windows shows a sense of the power of symmetry and axis — this also is part of the *natural order*. The living room has large french windows, arranged on centre, and this pattern is reinforced by the dropped cill line at each end of the equally symmetrical bedroom window directly below. (The only asymmetrical element of the facade is the Voyseyesque front door, keyed to the position of the staircase to one side.) The facades are deliberately formal. They suggest a familiarity not only with the Corbusier of the Schwob Villa at La-Chaux-de-Fonds, but also with Palladio's scheme for his own town house, which employs a blank panel on centre to accentuate the formality of conventional elements used at a modest scale.[10]

Taking note of the deliberate formality of this design, we must acknowledge the deliberate tensions which it sets out to create as between form and programme. It employs the bowler hat along with the unkempt hair, in a combination which has since become familiar in the garment system. Its audacity is not so much in presenting a house as a warehouse, as in presenting a warehouse as a creation of the mind. Its method is simultaneously to reverse polite tradition, while returning to an earlier and more fundamental civilization. It is bent, above all, on providing the evidence 'that men are at work'.

The same is true of Hunstanton School. But the Soho house is both more personal and more intense, intended as it was to be both a studio home and a studied manifesto. That it embodies the architects' serious intentions, however, and cannot be dismissed as a mere personal fantasy, can be seen from the presence of similar ideas in other early Smithson works of this period. For example, the extension to a house in Bayswater (ill. 3,4) is a modest commission, again confined by the limitations of parallel boundary walls. We find that the large windows facing the garden along the length of the new salon are accorded the formality of a cross-axis.

Again, in the Sugden house (ill. 5) of 1956 we see a similar preoccupation carried a step further. Here we have a modest suburban house which is almost by definition the essence of the humdrum, and which therefore invites comparison with the work of countless lowly professionals. It is built of traditional materials and has an open staircase leading out of the living room behind a free-standing fireplace in best Ideal Home manner. The annoyance it caused among practitioners derives from a sense of unease when facing the deliberate formality of the main elevation. Here the two L-shaped windows in the upper storey enhance a large square window to the living room. The elements are arranged in approximate although not in exact symmetry, like an oblique view of a familiar face. Indeed the facade verges on a physiognomic presence, and perhaps this is an additional reason why 'it was recognized by timid souls as a subtly subversive building'.[11]

That the building is serious, however, can be seen from its relationship to the Soho house. The elements disposed to create a deliberate effect are similar, if in the Soho house we can regard the run of bedroom window as being made up of two L-shaped units joined together, and enhancing the dominance of the square living room window placed above. These same elements are in the Sugden house more freely disposed. But by insisting on a measure of deliberate formality along with basic utility, they raise

3, 4. Alison & Peter Smithson. Extension to a house in Bayswater. 1959.
5. Alison & Peter Smithson. Sudgen house, Watford. 1956.
6. Alison & Peter Smithson. Garden Building, St Hilda's College, Oxford. 1969.

11

the stakes, stating an intention beyond simple utility and infusing banal material with unexpected interest.

The Smithsons' work, always premeditated, never unthinking, reflects a continual preoccupation with ideas and places. In their search for authenticity they do not pretend to answer the programme mechanically, but rather make a moral principle of their right to intervene. Thus they circle the problem of form, seeking to release the programme into a transcendental content. This search renders each fresh project unpredictable; a superficial view would suggest that they have many times changed direction. Certainly there are apparent contradictions, as for example between the modest craftmanship of the Soho and Sugden houses and the aggressive theoretical industrialization of their next step, in the projected 'house-of-the-future'. As later, in inverse direction between the gentle connected-ness of St Hilda's, Oxford (ill. 6), and the topological exactitude of their design for the University of Sheffield. Or between the casual restraint of the Economist group (pp. 181–183) and the strenuous rhetoric of their public housing in Hackney. These changes of stance are certainly opportunistic, but only in the sense that a satisfactory outlet for principles must be sought in life as it is found. To impose principles unfeelingly would be as wrong as to fail to connect the material as found to some transcendental framework, thus revealing in it a significance not previously realized. This is a dialectical approach. Each project represents a special outcome which has been felt into and thought out, a resolution of feeling and principles. It could be claimed that it is the Smithsons who, in the English scene, best respond to the image of a continuing Picturesque tradition projected by Pevsner.[12]

The Smithsons were afraid that architecture had been reduced to a level of mindless routine. They were ashamed that the calling of architect should mean so little in society while the philosopher, the scientist and the artist were honoured. By daring to admit to the non-professional content of their work, that is precisely that area which is not concerned with the status quo and its preservation, by daring to admit to having both feelings and principles, they reclaimed the potential of built form as a vehicle for ideas, and asserted the responsibility of the architect as an intellectual and artist. They were protesting, in effect, against the impoverishment of symbolic values in the architecture of the modern movement in England during the fifties.

It would be wrong to pretend that the Smithsons alone were responsible for the emergence of Brutalism as a second international style. They did make a vital contribution, however, to bringing Britain back into the mainstream of development. The fact that this development was directed towards an increasing degree of self-consciousness in the manipulation of form is not to be laid at their door. The problem of form exists, and their work has made it credible for an English architect to be concerned with it. This has been effected by their interest in the other arts, their lively polemic, their involvement with the death of CIAM (Congrès Internationaux d'Architecture Moderne), their teaching at the Architectural Association School (where Peter Smithson was for a time fifth year master) and their projects, built and unbuilt.[13] They can be said to have rescued English architecture from parochialism.

But they also contributed in no minor way to the predicament of architecture in the world scene. The theory of architecture which existed after the second world war was a debilitated functionalism. The issues of Stalinism versus the intellectual, of function as formal determinism or formal expression, had never been securely faced. The extent to which, and the conditions under which, architecture could be conceived as a rational process free from subjective prejudice had not been understood. To appreciate the place of British architecture in the Brutalist sixties it will be necessary to reconsider the theory of functionalism and to mark the reasons for its decline.

The decline of functionalism

The idea that the architect is a grand master, who is expected to introduce higher value into the fabric of the environment by means of the master-works he designs, is a common stereotype. Although it goes back to the Renaissance, it survived into the era of professionalism when it achieved a renewed, if conditional status. Lutyens, like his contemporary Elgar, was a grand master in this tradition, and his career was considered a model for students of the School of Architecture in Liverpool University right up to the second world war. However the trouble has been that, professionally speaking, the grand master is a charlatan. His success depends on offering a quality which is beyond price, for a price which his client can afford. He tends to see himself as a barrister rather than a solicitor, but much of the professional task of serving a client well lies at the humble level of providing value for money and reading the small print of the building contract. To be and to see oneself today as an architect with a responsibility to a higher vision demands an honesty and a sense of integrity which must look beyond the betterment of an individual client towards the betterment of society as a whole.

Modern architecture was conceived in the debates of small groups of artists and intellectuals in precisely these terms. The betterment of society was to be achieved by displacing the intermediary role of the architect as artist and adopting a rational concept which would allow the needs of society to be answered directly by the operation of an objective process. Thus from its inception modern architecture was infused with an egalitarian dream of escaping from personal vision and from higher values alike, so much had these become identified with the futilities and banalities of the ancien régime. The enthusiasts of the de Stijl, Purist, Futurist and Constructivist movements all had in common some idea of cleansing society, seizing reality directly, exposing necessity, and finding beauty in truth. Architecture indeed became 'modern' through an act of regeneration which was to make it different from all previous architecture. It was to be formally liberated from the problems and contradictions of style by abolishing style. Ornament was to become a crime. Architecture was no longer to serve the rulers, but the oppressed; it was to cease being an agent of repression and become instead the agent of liberation.

Whilst the grand masters of the first generation of modern architects — Wright, Mies, Le Corbusier — made no secret of their belief in their own personal vision, it is also true that they all suffered in varying degrees from uncertainty and paranoia, and found it necessary to justify their vision by arguments based on necessity. Le Corbusier, for instance, defended himself against a critic who had accused him of formalism by boasting that he had designed all the elevations for his League of Nations Design in three hours flat — so directly were they the result of the rational decisions taken in the plans and sections, already completed. He also stated, in order to make clear that he would not purvey the merchandise of accepted rhetoric, that he had specifically refused a commission to design a church.[14]

Thus for Le Corbusier as for lesser men, the ethos of modern architecture demanded a renunciation of accepted symbols. As far as possible and even when (as with Le Corbusier) there remained an avowed desire to forge new symbols, the form of buildings was to be exposed from within rather than imposed from without, that is the form was to be a rational reflection of the building programme. Philosophically speaking, the aim of functionalism was to release the necessities of the programme not into transcendental values, but into simple existence.

Of the theorists of functionalism, only Hannes Meyer (and he only for a short time) went so far as to reduce functionalism to pure utilitarianism, rejecting altogether the idea of symbolic content in a building. He claimed that architecture was not an art although it could have an artistic mission entrusted to it by society. In a statement written in 1931 as a manifesto of Marxist architecture, he includes the following points: 'Architecture is no longer the art of building. Building has become a science. Architecture is building science... The artistic mission of proletarian architecture is to produce organic architectural entities which lend themselves to the most varied manifestations of proletarian art; mass cinema, mass demonstrations, mass theatre, and mass sport... The building itself is not a work of art. Its size is determined by the dimensions and functions of its programme and not by the shallow pathos of any trimmings.'[15]

By 1938 he had adopted a less exposed position, but still insisted on the social contingency of architecture:

'The architect is an artist, for all art is a matter of organization; that is of reality shaped according to a new system... Like all the arts, architecture is a matter of public morals. The architect is fulfilling his moral function if he analyses his assignment with single-minded truthfulness and puts it into the form of a building honestly and boldly.'[16]

As Claude Schnaidt says, 'to open the path of progress what had to be discovered at all costs was the original technical and economic function of architecture. Anything that was not immediately and indisputably of use to the work had to be eliminated. Modern objectivity was to oust subjectivity, and the rational take the place of the arbitrary.'[17]

Hannes Meyer's achievement has been to inspire us with an ideal of a rational architecture in the service of man. He did not succeed, however, in arriving at such an architecture in his own work. The reasons why he did not succeed in this are not the result of his personal failure, they are rather philosophical. No one person can expect to change the language by a single effort of speech — his speech is always, and inevitably, compromised by the language.[18] Yet the language can be changed — by and through society — in a longer time cycle than the individual can encompass. Kenneth Frampton has shown us very clearly, in his comparison of the designs for the League of Nations by Hannes Meyer and Le Corbusier, that Le Corbusier's deliberate search for ritual expression did not prevent him from giving attention to utilities like air-conditioning and window cleaning; whereas Meyer's concern for utilitarian values did not prevent him from ignoring or leaving out precisely these elements of building service.[19] The attempts to achieve objectivity, therefore, are limited not by the degree of fulfillment of programmatic ends, but rather by the very function of communication, with its requirement that a fresh message can only be legible if it is conveyed in a code that is already established.

What Hannes Meyer was doing in his League of Nations design must be seen in relation to his own words, which contain the contradiction to which I wish to draw attention. 'Our League of Nations symbolizes nothing... As an organic building it expresses unfeignedly that it is intended to be a building for work and co-operation.'[20] Here the two aspects of functionalism, that in which function is the determinant of form, and that in which form is the expression of function, are hopelessly compounded. At this stage in the understanding of architecture and its role in society *it was not possible* as yet to separate them. In Meyer's approach symbolism in the form is denied, but idealization of the programme is affirmed. Since the form of the building, considered as a sign, relates signifier and signified, it is impossible to prevent its becoming suffused with symbolic content.[21] This happens at two levels: for the originator, in conceiving the form, and again for the observer, in receiving it.

I have suggested that architecture, as a form of expression, can be legitimately dealt with in terms of language. It is far from clear, however, whether architecture is a language in its own right — what meanings are specific to this language, or, indeed, if specific meanings can be conveyed at all purely through the medium of built form, and independently of words. But the fact is that we are never placed in a position of receiving a work of architecture without some form of words being offered as part of the transaction. At the two levels I have named, that of the originator and that of the observer, we are well served by the polemics of architects (they have all spoken) and the interpretations of critics. The forms of buildings are thereby drawn into the wider framework of language and culture, which is indeed a universal medium.

It is characteristic of new discovery that it is absorbed into common knowledge, and of fresh vision that it is deadened by acceptance. The cultural legacy is never complete, but it accumulates, and this accumulation is felt by the individual innovator as a weight from which he must free himself, through an effort of rejection, in order to be able to create afresh. The process of renewing our vision is not painless, it demands moral courage as well as creative vitality. Reason and emotion are both involved at the moment of insight.

'.... a man is a brain and a heart, reason and passion. Reason knows only the absolute of the science of the day, and passion is a living force which tends to carry along after it the objects which are available.'[22]

The division of heart and head, however, is a dichotomous one, the resultant of our analysis; in man they are inseparable, and at the creative moment they act together and invisibly. Yet they correspond, within the individual, to a more evident division of the material of life, to which his action is directed. This material is not only felt by the individual as external to him, it is so. It is an entire complex of material existence in flux which includes, for a short time, the designer as a living agent. However, also felt by the designer as external to him is the abstract complex of ideas, values, concepts, principles and games, which together make up the cultural legacy. These entities are immaterial, but they are present to his mind, and they also exist for others. Ernst Cassirer has named this the world of symbolic forms, and has suggested that it is an inescapable part of the environment of a man. It constitutes an immaterial but real part of the flux of existence by which each individual is surrounded and society sustained.

In a sense this mental furniture which humanizes the material universe is a web of illusion, as invisible as it is pervasive, infusing nature with the very qualities through which man endeavours to objectify and control it. The struggle for objectivity must therefore be understood in terms of intelligibility. For the innovator, a paradox results, which has been well stated by Ernst Cassirer:

'The forms in which life manifests itself and by means of which it acquires an objective form signify both a resistance to life and an indispensable support. If they present obstacles to it, it is obstacles through which it becomes conscious of its power and learns to use this power.'[23]

We may surmise that the variety of human experience, in the creative mode, is made up of the endless conflict between the balance of heart and head within the agent, and the balance of life and language in the perceptual content of his agency. Beyond this is the dialectic of history as it actually happens, the product of forces which include the forces within men's minds. The meeting place of these forces is the universe of forms, where the attempt is made simultaneously to objectify the forces and render them intelligible. Like speech, form (including the form of building) both articulates and mediates feeling and principles. Its role is essentially two-faced, and it is this ambiguity which produces for the architect what I have called the problem of form.[24]

In touching on these philosophical problems I am well aware that we are encroaching on a specialist field, and that there may be pitfalls in the way of trying to relate these abstruse matters to the simple practice of architecture, what is for most architects also – if not only – a way of earning a living. Yet I believe it has to be faced that many fields of human activity which appear to have been normalized, are increasingly open to analysis as the power and range of the human sciences increases. One penalty of this is a loss of innocence in rationalizing our actions.

Without seeking to apply superficial solutions to the subject of architectural design, I think we can at least envisage this activity in a wider context. I do not doubt that architecture, like clothes, is a kind of language system, capable of functioning simultaneously as a utility and as a means of expression. That buildings, considered as architectural statements, cannot be meaningless (although their meaning can be trite) and that the form of buildings, however and in whatever degree determined by programmatic considerations, will be found more than programmatically significant, both as offering and as happening. Success in rationalizing the building programme and the building form – which at present is the subject of research with computers – will not in my opinion remove the problem of form, although it will undoubtedly shift it into new aspects.

What we are concerned with here is limited to the change in architects' attitudes to the concept of functionalism, and the gradual realization, in the whole immediate postwar period up to 1954 (in England at least) that the redemptive qualities of the functionalist approach, so ardently looked for in 1929, had proved to be an illusion. It was not after all possible to arrive at an architecture which would transparently transmit the content of the building task and no other content.

During the fifties, as we have seen, a new impulse was given to the movement to reassert the role of the architect as an interpreter of the brief and an innovator in the realm of form. The impulse was largely expressed through the writings and work of the Smithsons, but it took its strength from a new generation of architects whose education was completed after the second world war, and who consequently looked back to the pre-war period of the international style with the eyes of discovery. For them the most important thing about the idea of modern architecture was not its freedom from style, but its potentiality as style. It was no longer possible to believe in a rational architecture without symbolic content. But the functionalist tradition, which had stressed the social contingency of architecture along with its theoretical rationalism, left architects with a bad conscience when it came to conscious manipulation of symbolic form. Throughout the fifties in England there reigned an uneasy truce between the empiricists and the idealogues. The Architectural Review, as we have seen, provided a rationale for the Picturesque style which, for all its scholarship and its cultivated sense of appropriate character, had been accompanied by a general feeling of drift and of missed purpose. Labels were invented to identify new movements which might resolve the moral dilemma posed by the recognition that form is wilful and ambiguous – the New Eclecticism, the New Humanism, the New Empiricism, finally the New Brutalism. With Brutalism the architect faced the moral dilemma with a response which at last recognized his own wilful nature. Reversing a precept of Mies van der Rohe, he said, in effect, 'I don't want to be good, I want to be interesting.'[25]

British architecture in the decade of the sixties is the direct result of this change of heart.

The manipulation of form

We have seen that Hannes Meyer, having at one time attempted to define architecture as building science, ended by admitting that it was after all an art. In the last resort he had to agree that scientific objectivity could not be achieved in it; but at least the aims of the programme should be pursued with single-minded determination, and translated into built form directly and honestly. We can concede, I think, that Hannes Meyer was successful in adopting this approach in his own work, and its quality depends on an evident sincerity, considering his life, his writings, and his built work as a composite expression of his spirit.

An interesting question arises, however, as to whether this sincerity is an inescapable part of the man, or can be applied at a level of methodology. Can sincerity be cultivated? Coming back to the two acts of interpretation which surround the built form – that of the architect who proposes it, and that of the observer, or user, who disposes of it – can one ask of the architect that he should confine himself sincerely to the first act, leaving the second act (that of the observer) to take care of itself? Or alternatively, knowing that the form of the building will be scanned for clues as to its meaning, is he not entitled, quite sincerely, to select a form or set of forms, which will convey to the observer as far as possible a true idea of the meaning of the building and of its programme?

Ideally we could postulate a situation where the architect may be able to translate the programme into form so single-mindedly and exhaustively that the form would become, in practical terms, a true if independent indication of the programme. The user of the building might then be enabled with comparative ease, and working only from the form of the building as experienced by him, to interpret correctly the meaning of the building – thus by a symmetrical but inverse process to that of the architect arriving back again at an understanding of the programme by means of the form. In this question, the content of the form would coincide *sufficiently* with the content of the programme to be able to stand effectively for it like a sign in language: the meaning of the building could be its programme.

It may indeed be claimed that this is the common-sense view of architecture as a social service: according to this view, buildings provide appropriate shelter, protection and so on, and *at the same time,* like clothes, provide appropriate character, the symbolic function and the utilitarian function going together hand in glove. This was the role of architecture as seen by Walter Gropius. Whereas Hannes Meyer's interpretation of architecture was little known, until the publication of Schnaidt's book in 1965, Gropius' ideas have been disseminated very widely, particularly through his role as teacher and educator, at the Bauhaus and in America. It is the functionalism of form as expression, and it can be argued that while architects invariably state that their form has been determined by the programme, what they really mean, and what they are doing, is to select forms which should be representative of the programme. Indeed, an honest pursuit of the programme, it could be argued, will include the selection of appropriate forms as part of the general appropriation of resources to satisfy needs.

However, we cannot escape, even in this commonsense view, from certain philosophical and political pitfalls. The question of what is rational and intelligible must now be restated in terms of what is appropriate and acceptable. Argument as to rationality and intelligibility can be conducted on a basis of logic; but arguments as to appropriateness and acceptability cannot be conducted without reference to prevailing values, which in this case means an entire Pandora's box of more or less conflicting values, reflecting the division of society as much as its common elements.

It was indeed the recognition that different elements in society would have irreconcilable views as to what should be considered appropriate, in a given situation, which brought the single-minded international style to a halt. Stalin's intervention was, from his point of view, quite logical: he asked only that building should satisfy *his* idea of what the man-in-the-street would consider appropriate. To paraphrase Meyer, the Warsaw Palace of Culture expresses unfeignedly that it is a place for work and cooperation, is a gift of the good Stalin to his children, and bears witness to the friendly and watchful power of the great Soviet Union. However much we may regret Stalin's taste in architecture, we have to concede that he had a straight understanding of the power of architecture to transmit ideas and of the need to gather it into the control of the state.

Can we really claim that Stalin's use of architecture as deliberate symbolism is any more reprehensible than that of any business corporation that erects a monument to

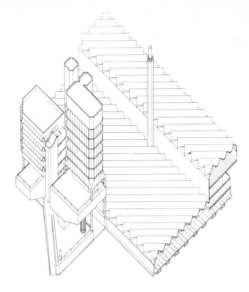

7. James Stirling, James Gowan. Engineering laboratories at Leicester University. 1960.

its own prestige? The Seagram Building, in New York, is widely praised as the most beautiful skycraper in that city. It does not advertise whiskey. But, as with the Warsaw tower, it aims to be impressive in a language that the citizens will understand. To each city its own dialect, and sense of the appropriate. The Palace of Culture, had it been erected in New York in 1929, would not have been particularly out of place. One of the penalties of Stalin's interpretation of symbols is that he was old-fashioned. This brings us to a second consideration — that of time as well as place. All societies change, at some times more quickly than at others. And there is a particular value to be placed on those elements in society which are concerned with the adaptation to change. In a sense this is everybody's affair, since each individual experiences change through his own ageing body, with its continual balance between the known past and the unknown future. The values of society reflect an urge for novelty as well as an urge for security, and it is inevitable that architecture should find itself, as with all other arts, suspended between past and future. Appropriateness of character in a building is compounded of both familiar and unfamiliar elements, and it is the particular balance of these elements in a building design which makes it both recognizable and interesting. If architects, through a change of heart, decide to be interesting, they will find themselves launched in a game in which the penalty will be dullness (with the advantage of obviousness) and the prize will be to force a reconsideration of the obvious, thus extending the repertoire for everyone. But this prize will only be won if the insight is strong enough to carry the obvious before it. Otherwise the result will be pretentious, or it may even reduce architecture merely to the pursuit of the fashionable.

It is at this point that a problematical element re-enters the situation. Considered as an art, architecture has a certain *gravitas*. Once this gave it its role as mistress of the arts. Today, when other arts have increasingly found autonomy as separate media of expression, architecture remains more than ever tied to the utilitarian purposes of buildings. Considered as a medium, it is somewhat elephantine. Can it really be disposed of freely as a simple means of expression? Could an architect readily admit to treating it as such? Remember how shocked we were when Philip Johnson built his miniature loggia at New Canaan — a pavilion whose social purpose was no more serious than the entertainment of his private guests. Few architects have been willing to expose themselves to possible charges of frivolity or irresponsibility. If they exercise an art, and manipulate form, they do so largely on the quiet, behind the cover of a functionalist ethic or, at least, methodology.

It is in this tradition of the programme as justification that Le Corbusier, some twenty-five years after he had turned down a commission to design a church because of the arbitrary use of symbols it would involve, could accept a commission for the design of a pilgrimage chapel. In Ronchamp the very original employment of symbolic forms is justified at every turn by topographical requirements which fix the external form and, internally, by plastic manipulation to exploit the emotional impact of controlled and reflected natural light. In the same vein, we find an English architect of the stature of James Stirling justifying chamfers at Leicester University (ill. 7; pp. 116–118) by reference to the pressure of a future road line cutting the corner of his site. Or we find John Weeks justifying a dominant pattern of staggered vertical mullions (pp. 132–134) by reference to a rationale of indeterminate accommodation of structural loads and weight distribution. The best, and perhaps the unanswerable, justification for a formal solution is the statement that it responds to a specific requirement of the client.

The client as actor

An ancient world-view has the earth carried on the back of an elephant standing on the shell of a tortoise swimming in a nameless sea. The difficulty of explaining how the universe is sustained is relegated to the end of a series. Whatever lies beyond him, the client has now taken on some of the aspects of this elephant in the world-view of the architect. A great deal can be blamed on him — his back is broad — while at the same time he exerts a sustaining role. If a true objectivity is elusive, and if an architect cannot be sure what meaning will be pinned on his built work by the critic, he can at least enter into a specific understanding with his client, so that the client's requirements, and his own intentions, can be brought into harmony. This contract may vary in the degree to which it imposes constraints on the architect's freedom. It need not preclude a wilful impulse nor deflect his moral urge to be of service to society rather than to an individual. The good client is expected to understand and support such endeavours. Since this contract is negotiated, it is likely that the job will not go forward at all unless some such understanding has first been reached.

The architect who can take his client's brief, restructure it in accordance with his own system of values, and then carry the client along with him in his proposals, has to some extent at least evaded the problem of form. He may mystify his client, or persuade him by rational argument, or convince him by a demonstration of a predictive model; but at least he will have the chance to achieve some degree of rapprochement between the content of the brief and the content of the built form. The initial concepts, whether of brief or of form, will have gone through a restructuring process over time; and through this process of consultation the final design, like a draft treaty, will be approved by both parties. Ambiguities may remain, by intention or oversight, and it does not follow that the client, when he eventually gets his building, will not be surprised, pleasantly or unpleasantly, nor does it follow that the building will in practice conform to his requirements, much less that it will respond adequately to the needs of the actual users. To achieve success all down the line requires a degree of predictive science on both sides of the bargain. The main thing, though, is that a bargain is struck.

There was a time when the architect stood on his dignity as an artist. He was approached by clients and offered commissions, and his business was to tell the client what his needs really were and what he could afford. Sir Edwin Lutyens and Frank Lloyd Wright behaved like this. Many architects continue to see themselves as offering a unique vision (a few indeed do). But not many today are so inflexible as to refuse to modify their initial concept, expecting an all-or-nothing acquiescence from the client.

In exchange for his greater flexibility, the architect expects to be permitted and enabled to penetrate the client's requirements, seeking to find a more fundamental structure in the data than would be possible if the brief were a peremptory one. The particularity of the client's needs is both a source of fresh ideas and to some extent an alibi. Insofar as the brief is not a priori self-evident it calls forth an effort of research and analysis, and it is here that the architect hopes to discover a basis for his design which will put him beyond criticism, and justify him as a source of creative ideas.

At the same time, his success in persuading the client, by whatever means, constitutes a quasi-objective 'proof' of the usefulness of his product and of its value outside the purely subjective realm. He has taken the opportunity of accommodating his own aspirations and scruples. Above all, his contract with the client reconciles for him his role as artist and as professional. It is normally only with the protection and full confidence of his client that the architect can 'let himself go'. The client legitimizes his wilfulness. The client in turn gains a great deal. He is enabled to undertake a systematic examination of his own requirements, including his current methods and mode of operation. He may be able to study the implications of different resolutions of his problems insofar as they are affected by the form of the building. The design of the building may turn out to be an important factor in the overall management of his affairs. To whatever level of interference he permits the architect, the client is able to enter the process of design, not as a simple patron, but as an actor in the play.

According to the values of society, the contract between client and architect can be conceived in different ways. There are clearly possibilities of conflict if the architect is not prepared to accept his client as he finds him. He may need to re-cast the whole form of society in order to satisfy the terms of a legitimate outlet for his skill. We have seen how, in order to establish a framework for an 'objective' architecture, Hannes Meyer had first to define the form of a just socialist society and the place of architecture in it. To a lesser degree architects who accept their clients and the opportunities they bring without wishing to change society first still need to believe in the social value of their work, and the renovative quality of their skill.

Even at the height of the Renaissance the architect attempted to set against his servitude to the king his independence as an artist. His understanding of the laws of architecture was claimed to go beyond arbitration — like the priest's special access to the laws of God. Bernini gave a marvellous performance on these lines. But when the personal vision of the architect was un-negotiable, he risked losing all; even the great Vanbrugh lost his client's confidence at one point, as we may see from the vengeful comments of Sara, Duchess of Marlborough on architects:

'I know of none that are not mad or ridiculous, and I really believe that anybody that has sense with the best workmen of all sorts could make a better house without an architect, than any has been built these many years.'[26]

8. J. L. Womersley. Park Hill, Sheffield. 1961.

The priestly nature of the architect's aspirations, and his attempt to define for himself an independent seat close to the source of power, were more clearly recognized in the French system than anywhere else. There, the Academy long supplied the architects for the state, and the Ecole des Beaux-Arts until very recently maintained this supply, exercising a competitive selection by means of the annual Prix de Rome. But in England, in spite of the great Wren, the architect (perhaps fortunately) has never achieved this compelling status. Here, where the industrial revolution first took hold, the nineteenth century saw an unprecedented growth in private construction of all kinds, and with it an expansion of the supply of what I would call architectural tradesmen, at many levels of expertise and initiative. The schools of architecture in England were only half-heartedly modelled on the French system (an English Prix de Rome was not established until 1912, already too late),[27] and were in fact dominated by the self-help attitudes and demands of the articled assistants. It was this group which was responsible for founding the Architectural Association and its school, a school which has since become virtually a world model for the self-help teaching institution as an educational concept, and which has certainly leavened the institutionalism of all schools of architecture in Britain.

This pluralist tradition was confirmed through the laissez-faire policies adopted by the Royal Institute of British Architects. Although concerned with creating and maintaining professional standards, it has chosen to do this through a relatively flexible and long-range set of controls. This has allowed the schools to develop independent educational policies, each recognized as 'giving exemption' from the centralized examination system, which is by now practically defunct. Today in Britain we find no less than 20,000 registered architects in a total population of 56 million, with as many again of architectural assistants. That means an architect to every 1500 people.[28] At the same time architects are in some way concerned in over 75% of building construction undertaken.[29] These figures indicate how common architects are in the country at large. Although the statistics cover the entire range of roles, some with high responsibility, some without, they do suggest a diffusion of skills and opportunities. About half of all architects are in the private sector. It is against this background that we must assess the very great importance, in Britain, of the personal transaction between architect and client as the source of power.

However, the simple availability of architects does not account for the range and diversity of the buildings which we see. Along with it we have to consider the function of management. Clearly, in the evolution of a more interactive relationship between client and architect, we cannot overlook the concurrent development of a professional skill in management, on both sides of design. This interface takes effect at the level of the top executive class in both client and design organizations.

I have already mentioned the importance of C. H. Aslin at the Hertford County Education Authority. Through his initative a rationalized technology for building schools was hitched to a liberal education programme in a single management policy. Also noteworthy, as establishing what is effectively a role of sponsor of design, have been the careers of Robert Matthew and of Leslie Martin as successive heads of the Architect's Department at London's County Hall, or of J. L. Womersley who as City Architect of Sheffield sponsored the Park Hill Development. There are many other cases where official architects who have risen into a position of executive power have liberally promoted the design efforts within their organizations, thus showing an understanding of the importance of their function, not only as producers, but as managers and interpreters of building design.

On the client side, one might mention, merely as an example, the notable case of the collaboration between Lord James, for the University, and Andrew Derbyshire (of Robert Matthew, Johnson-Marshall and Partners) in evolving a radical brief for the University of York, permitting an extensive use of a standard technology based on CLASP. Or note the enthusiasm with which Professor Parkes, as then head of department, welcomed Stirling and Gowan's strenuous design for the Engineering Faculty Building at Leicester University, seeing in it a happy union of practical and symbolic values; or note the response of the board of the *Economist* newspaper, who, having set a competition for a single building, were quick to see the advantage in the Smithsons' solution which offered them three. There are indeed many examples in British architecture of imaginative intervention by institutional clients in the promotion of building programmes. The client, like the architect, is frequently instructed by a set of ideals which look beyond the immediate satisfaction of his own requirements to a wider responsibility to society. In these good intentions he is to some degree prodded by the planning controls residual from the 1947 Planning Act. Although public ownership of the development value of land has never been effectively implemented, the recognition of public rights in the overall impact of redevelopment has undoubtedly played a part in moderating the exploitation of land, as may be seen by comparing the situation in Britain with that in other countries where public interests are assigned a minor status.

This said, it remains broadly true that the public at large are excluded from the contract between architect and client, which like the administration of justice, involves expert handling and expert evidence. How insidious this professional expertise is can be seen from an example like the Park Hill development at Sheffield (ill. 8). The architects here were strongly imbued with social responsibility, and anxious to avoid or reduce the social alienation sometimes thought insuperable in public housing estates. In Park Hill, the street deck advocated by the Smithsons in their Golden Lane Competition entry is developed, independently, with the advantages of a sloping site which permits all levels of public circulation to connect to ground naturally at one end. In this concept they hoped to retrieve, in flatted development, the cooperative values of the street. The social adjuncts of shops and clinics and so on have been dutifully attached to the scheme, and the elevations have been given a tough yet dignified aspect void of 'the shallow pathos of any trimmings' (to use Meyer's phrase). They are studiedly underdesigned. Yet we must wonder whether they constitute a human environment for ordinary people. Like the Regency terraces at Bath or Bristol, they produce magnificent skylines. Unlike the Regency terraces, however, they were not freely chosen by the people who went to live in them. Uncomfortably, we are impressed by their grandiosity. As architecture, they are formidable. Can we deny that they embody, however unwillingly, a tradition of rhetoric which goes back through Le Corbusier to Fourier and through Nash to Ledoux? It is the rhetoric which makes a palace out of a place.

The uses of rhetoric

Roland Barthes defines rhetoric as belonging to a secondary level of language (along with metalanguage), where the elements which are employed as signifiers are already in their own right complete signs at a primary or purely denotative level. This secondary level, when it is not a metalanguage, he calls connotative, and the signifiers he calls connotators. The medium they constitute is a rhetoric, and the content they offer is a fragmented ideology, made up of the many individual things signified:
'These "signifieds" have a very close communication with culture, knowledge, and history, and it is through them, so to speak, that the environmental world invades the system (of language). We might say that *ideology* is the form of the signifieds of connotators, while *rhetoric* is the form of the connotators.'[30]
Barthes goes on to show that both metalanguage and connotative discourse are common elements in our everyday use of language: a fashion magazine, in discussing clothes, may well employ both levels, one on top of the other, as well as the simple denotative level of pointing to particular objects of discussion. The extent to which we may slip, unknowingly, from one level of language to another, even in scientific discourse, is a source of common confusion, and explains why the language of formal logic, which is governed by exact rules, is so different from ordinary speech. In the language of advertising, on the other hand, the rhetorical content is plainly exposed, whether in hard sell or soft sell mode.
Rhetoric is language used as persuasion. Through its system of connotations, a fragmented ideological content is assembled and uttered as speech. To judge by history, architecture is an animal of this sort.
At the very opening of the sixties, Reyner Banham published his book on the architecture of the machine age.[31] In it he says some hard things about architects, pointing to the discrepancies between what they said and what they did; his exposure of functionalism as merely another style was hard to take, particularly as he himself continues to look to a 'really' functional architecture of the future. Yet in justice it must be said that functionalism did not die only by Banham's axe: it was already close to dissolution in the corrosive ferment of Brutalism. Although functionalism was in theory directed towards a purely denotative level of content, based on a prior appeal to reason, logic and economy, in practice it never succeeded in purifying itself of connotative levels of reference. Banham has shown us the depth and complexity of symbolism attached

to the 'pure' forms of functionalism by analysing in detail two generally accepted functionalist masterpieces — Le Corbusier's Villa at Poissy, 'Les Heures Claires' and Mies' Barcelona Pavilion. In the latter case he concludes:

'It is clear that even if it were profitable to apply strict standards of rationalist efficiency or functionalist formal determinism to such a structure, most of what makes it architecturally effective would go unnoticed in such an analysis.'[32]

The sense of architectural form as being, like language, inherently and yet incoherently fragmented with meaning, has finally entered into the awareness of the modern architect. Among those who are worried by the syntagmatic potential of architectural form, that is by its potential of cohering into *architecturally effective* assemblages, some react by directing their attention from the thing (the signifier) to the idea (the signified) seeking an ideological determinism which will justify the form; others react by concentrating on the thing-ness of the sign — the building as object — seeking for justification at the level of primary, or denotative meaning, that is in the determinism offered by the details of the programme. Both of these attitudes are doomed to failure, philosophically speaking, but insofar as they propose a concern which is separate from the actual means of persuasion involved, they may produce a state of mind which is not too consciously manipulative. It is the fear of being suspected of conscious manipulation of form, in the sense of persuasive rhetoric, that haunts the honest architect and leads him to deny the inescapable rhetorical content of his favourite forms. For Peter Smithson, buildings like the Chandigarh Secretariat or the Chase Manhattan Bank in New York are without rhetoric, because they display their true nature, but without ostentation. 'In my view, the invention of the formal means whereby we sense the essential presence only — without display or rhetoric — of the mechanisms which of necessity support and service our buildings, is the very heart of architecture at present. To make our mechanisms speak with our spaces, is our central problem.'[33]

But the problem of speech in architecture, whether of mechanisms or of space, is inseparable from the nature of language. To praise one's favourite buildings because they are 'without rhetoric' is to mistake ends for means, acquiescing in their ideological values in order to allow the primary level of their denotative values to speak directly to one's feelings. The problem of speech and the nature of language, however, carry us willy-nilly into the realm of social values, as Smithson himself has constantly pointed out. The whole effort of Team 10 was directed at discovering those forms, or that set of forms, which would operate as physical mechanisms, bringing order and functional efficiency to the city, while *at the same time* displaying themselves sufficiently to be visible, to be comprehensible, to the citizen, and to provide for him a public framework of orientation and identity. The opening section of the Team 10 Primer states:

'Each period requires a constituent language — an instrument with which to tackle the human problem posed by the period, as well as those which, from period to period, remain the same, i. e. those posed by man — by all of us as a primordial being. The time has come to gather the old into the new; to rediscover the archaic qualities of human nature, I mean the timeless ones.'[34]

As we have seen, Le Corbusier from the beginning was aware of the poetic inheritance of architecture as something which had to be re-invented, according to the contingencies of the period, but always so as to preserve and provide solace for certain inextinguishable human aspirations and needs – *les constants humains.*[35] In Le Corbusier's masterpieces a level of poetic expression is reached which we can recognize as universal. Not all his work, however, reached the level of lyrical intensity of 'Les Heures Claires', and episodes like the Algiers skyscraper of 1938–42, or (to take Smithson's own example) the articulation of the suites belonging to the top executives in the Chandigarh Secretariat building, reveal clearly the underlying rhetorical devices on which he based his vocabulary of form. Any architect who sets out to articulate the expectation of ordinary human beings in the public realm (and which will say that he does not?) will encounter the problem of how to combine the universal with the particular. Rhetoric, as the art of the public realm, imposes a plurality of values corresponding perfectly in its degree of complexity with the social structure of the culture. There are all kinds of rhetoric, and we will often feel that most of it is bad. It is this problem which Robert Venturi endeavours to solve by an architecture which simultaneously embodies two levels of rhetoric — a popular rhetoric for the common man, and an arcane rhetoric for his friends the knowing critics. He thereby tries to counter the elitist trends in American architecture, practised by architects like Johnson and Rudolph, which had split the profession into two.[36]

9, 10. Skidmore, Owings & Merrill; Yorke Rosenberg Mardall. Boots head office, Nottingham. 1966.

9

10

Let us turn to a few examples of the gentle art of persuasion, as practised in England. Our first, that of the Boots head offices (ill. 9, 10), issues from the American office of Skidmore, Owings and Merrill with its English equivalent Yorke Rosenberg Mardall as supervising architects. This is one of those deceptively simple buildings, in the Mies tradition of 'less is more', which we might describe as the soft sell. The building reveals its structure, and is hardly anything more than its structure. The denotative significance of the simple steel frame is immediately apparent. This directness may have rhetorical repercussions of a higher order — but surely it falls within the Meyerist call for honesty? Is it not a statement devoid of 'the shallow pathos of any trimmings'? For the innocent it may be honest. But with some knowledge of the historical context, its meaning becomes more specific. This building must be seen as the successor of the giant skyscraper of Chicago. It turns the large-scale structure to advantage, in a single-storey building, where the strength of the span implies a flexibility of the space, a built-in capability for managerial change and rearrangement. This quality is also denotatively true. But it carries an inescapable connotation of power in reserve, appropriate to the image of a grand corporation with multiple assets. The rhetoric is restrained, but unequivocal: the architecture is recognizably a giant order. The head office is also a palace.

In Centre Point (ill. 11) we may see a rhetoric almost devoid of artifice. Richard Seifert is an architect of great business acumen, who has made himself the master of the regulations limiting building volume by plot area. He knows how to extract the largest, and hence most profitable, office block from the limitations of a given site. He does not need to persuade his clients by rhetoric — his figures are convincing in themselves. Whereas most so-called skyscrapers sited in London have histories of being chopped down in size, and therefore look stumpy, this one has something of the soaring grace of the Pirelli Building in Milan (of 1960). Like Meyer's League of Nations, this tower expresses unfeignedly that this is a place for work and economic advantage. Only in the fancy legs and the self-conscious engineer's shaping of the precast facade units do we detect a lack of savoir-faire, which we may choose to regard as an error of taste. Even in this aspect, however, the building is a perfect symbol of the commercial world which brought in into being.

Nothing if not tasteful is the now famous addition to Brasenose College (ill. 12), by Powell and Moya. Here is an attempt to make an architecture of discretion, recognizably modern, but capable of slipping unobtrusively into the venerable environment of Oxford. Real stone, real lead, are used, and the scale of the volumes is broken down into house-sized units so that the regular repetition of windows floor by floor does not read as too mechanical. The necessary connotations for social acceptability are thus achieved through the use of familiar materials and forms: but the vocabulary still transmits its allegiance to the architecture of white walls and flat roofs, and of rational repetition. This is a rhetoric of reconciliation.

The Brasenose addition heralded a fantastic proliferation of collegiate architecture in the universities, both old and new. The fifties had been dominated by school building: now it was the turn of higher education, and the opportunity for architects who could aspire to higher things. Socially speaking, the time was ripe for an expansion of higher education, which had lagged terribly in Britain compared with other developed countries. Part of the ripeness was in the realization that the modern style in architecture was not inescapably proletarian, that it was adaptable, that it could conform. The discovery was equally valid whether it was a matter of adjusting to an established environment of privilege, or of creating in some green field a recognizable 'university' ambience. Architect and client together suddenly grasped the potential of architecture to express and articulate the social realm, creating all degrees of environment from community to privacy, from participation to exclusiveness. Together they settled down to exploit the uses of rhetoric.

Credibility and ambiguity

In the Cripps Building at St John's College, Cambridge (pp. 86, 87), the same architects who had been so successful at Brasenose were asked to do a much grander job. Again they had to produce a building which would blend into a varied array of old buildings surrounding the site and which would, like them, last five hundred years. They have achieved these objectives by similar means, with Portland stone as a general facing, breaking down the scale by means of a profile varied in both plan and section, and

11

12

11. Richard Seifert. Centre Point, London. 1961.
12. Powell and Moya. Addition to Brasenose College, Oxford. 1959.
13, 14. Chamberlin, Powell & Bon. New Hall, Cambridge. 1962.

creating collegiate courtyards in combination with the existing buildings out of a single spine which bends back and forth in easy stages. The new building does fit into its surroundings without entirely sacrificing its credibility as white-walled modern architecture. But the credibility is strained. The reconciliation it effects with the external environment is achieved only with some degree of internal contradiction and a doubt as to its own identiy. Its five hundred years of life expectancy weigh more heavily than do five hundred years of past history in its surroundings. Would we not have been better off to have gone all the way into explicit eclecticism, with an arbitrary but suitable choice of historical precedent? In a New World setting, the collegiate Gothic of the Princeton University campus dates only from about 1910, but its authenticity, deriving from the deliberate historicism of its own moment, is entirely convincing.

With New Hall, Cambridge (ill. 13, 14), the crisis of identity reaches a more acute level. Here the architects (Chamberlin, Powell & Bon) were faced with the other end of the problem: how to make something out of nothing. They had to create a college on a suburban site. Instead of joining externally to a settled scene, the building has to make its own scene within the confines of the spaces it can itself enclose. The problem of character is not how to blend new with old, but how within the category of the entirely new, and with all the constraints of normal construction costs, to secrete some nucleus of pomp and circumstance which will focus attention and persuade us of our unique destiny. Within the complex of residential rooms, common rooms, library and dining hall this added quality (which we might call a projected diachronous dimension) is identified by the use of curved forms, not normally required for economic construction, and therefore indicating an intention going beyond that of utility. The play of curves against planes takes various forms — circular fountains, arches, vaults, cupolas and a dome. In the general structure of the plan a sense of climax is achieved by the predominance accorded to the dining hall, with its high central dome and its attendant group of four cupola-topped staircases standing around it like minarets. The forcing of the rhetoric is plain enough: we are left in no doubt that we are under persuasion. But what is the specific message?

The connotations seem to be a combination of historical, functional and psychological. We are reminded of Renaissance church, governor's mansion, Turkish mosque. There is a distinct suggestion of royal observatory or of nuclear fission. In Freudian terms we may see a reference, appropriate in a women's college, to the special place of feminine curves in a rigid men's world. However, none of these allusions may be particularly important, when measured against the ample fact that the form employed is rich enough to suggest any or all of them: it is its very portentousness which is valued — the fact that the building is more than matter-of-fact; denoting its function as a college, but connoting also a perspective of other possibilities which bracket the prime meaning into quotation marks. This building does not simply demonstrate, unfeignedly, what it is for. It imposes a kind of make-believe. This we may find somewhat incredible in a building, although accepting it as a matter of course in the more consumptive display of clothes, cars and food which we encounter daily.

New Hall is a clear case of formalism — the form manipulated quite freely in the service of the rhetoric. The possibilities of this approach are infinite, but one would like to think that they have been carried to a logical conclusion, in theory at least, in the work of a student at the Architectural Association school, who proposed a form of vacation housing based on modular units of structure produced by high technology.[37] On to these basic units separate skins, providing interior and exterior faces, may be clipped. These are available in a whole range of 'characters', from primitive hut to bomb-proof shelter, from period to modern; like the basic structure, they would be mass-produced, cheap and expendable. The choice they offer is the choice we already exercise with cars or clothes, with which we keep warm, go places, and have fun. The system would permit houses to join in the spectacle of conspicuous consumption and instant recognition.

But in the design of buildings to house social institutions, we cannot so readily tolerate expendable symbols. We still stop short at the idea of the building itself taking part in the scenic transformations. Our response to the building as a vehicle of rhetoric is conditional on its apparent neutrality. Once revealed as being itself a performance, its rhetoric becomes a paper tiger — it has to be enduring, however monstrous, to be authentic. Even in the transformation scenes proposed by Cedric Price, as for example in his Fun Palace, a mechanism of large-scale structure, complete with cranes, is accorded a permanent role of *deus ex machina,* supporting and making possible

13

14

15

15. Richard Sheppard, Robson & Partners. Churchill College, Cambridge. 1960.
16. Richard Sheppard, Robson & Partners. Linstead Hall, Imperial College, London. 1960.
17. Arup Associates. George Thompson Building, Corpus Christi College, Cambridge. 1963.

16

17

the scenic transformations, but outside of them. The solution of withdrawing the essential structure from the game is probably due to a sense of the *gravitas* of architecture, of its being too serious a matter to joke with. We may remember that Hannes Meyer wanted at one time to withdraw architecture from the field of art, while allotting to it the artistic mission of providing a neutral setting for displays of popular culture. However, for a building to function as the shell for an institution it has to combine within itself an element of continuity, even of permanence, and an element too of responsiveness, so that the evolution of social values may be satisfied in both diachronous and synchronous dimensions. It is the attempt to combine both dimensions in a single entity which gives so much of the architecture of the sixties its evidently self-conscious stance.

The problem becomes most acute — to the English cast of mind, most embarrassing — when an effort has to be made to stage a traditional scene, like the college dinner, without recourse to explicit eclecticism. It is no accident that the majority of colleges designed in the sixties make the dining hall into the centrepiece of the plan — a position which used to be filled by the chapel. Chapels have become smaller, and dining halls larger, and the ritual of dining in hall touches most of the college community. So an effort is made, at least once in each project, to match the permanence of traditional building by a display of modern formality, coincidental with the function of spanning the largest space.

A degree of uncertainty in the credibility of its rhetoric is noticeable in Churchill College (ill. 15) by Richard Sheppard, Robson & Partners. This design was the winner in an open competition, which included some interesting essays in extended rhetoric; but it was indeed among the more modest solutions, and has been widely praised for its restraint and realism. It offers a decent modicum of formality within the limits of a tight budget. The residential accommodation is grouped in small courtyards of two or three storeys, the upper storeys being freely varied by projecting bay windows. The scale is domestic and the 'more monumental central buildings' are inflated beyond the three storey limit only by the addition of arched clerestories and the exposed supporting beams. The style is a modified Brutalism, with horizontal bands of brick alternating with the concrete slab edges; more like Stirling and Gowan's Ham Common flats than the Maison Jaoul. The rhetoric is decidedly low-key, and inoffensive. It is a case rather of discretion being the better part of valour, with the penalty that the result is nothing like so memorable as, say, Basil Spence at Sussex (where one feels that valour has had the better of discretion). Nor does it evince any of the bravado exhibited in the halls of residence for Imperial College, London (ill. 16), erected simultaneously by the same architects in a style more homogeneously derivative. This design is straightforwardly in the manner of an urban *unité d'habitation* and consequently a safer vehicle altogether. This example helps us to understand the advantages and limitations of working within an accepted style. The style, being already defined, offers the reassurance of a species of greatcoat, transforming even small men into handsome guardsmen. The rhetoric, which is already syntagmatically composed, is instantly recognizable and elicits a set response. It leaves nothing to be puzzled out. At least, in Churchill, the architects are inventing their rhetoric as they go along, and making use of whatever comes to hand, like the need for larger spans. Even the air extract housings, on the

18. Llewelyn-Davies Weeks Forestier-Walker & Bor. Laboratories for the Zoological Society, London. 1963.
19. Michael Brawne. House at Fisher's Pond. 1964.
20. Sir Basil Spence, Bonnington & Collins. Union building, University of Southampton. 1964.

gables of the dining hall, have been given a deliberate, if enigmatic, significance, by the exact symmetry of their positioning.

One way of dignifying the architecture without the need to resort to special treatment in particular parts is by upgrading the structural elements throughout. At Corpus Christi, Cambridge (ill. 17), we have one of many examples by Arup Associates in which this approach is adopted. Time and attention have been given to the design of the basic unit of structure, usually — as here — in precast concrete. The units fit together in a clearly articulated assembly, and in the aggregate build up a comprehensive structural framework which is at the same time functional and visual. By this means a certain systematic engineering determinism is inserted into the rhetoric, providing a rationale and a justification.

The architects Howell, Killick, Partridge and Amis are particularly successful proponents of the elegant precast structure. Their buildings are evidently in the mainstream of Brutalist expressionism, but the brutality is so subdued by the sophistication of the technology that it comes over polite, like a voice which, though loud, has the right accent. These are buildings which manage to look expensive without looking dishonest. Among the prettiest is their residential group at St Anne's, Oxford (pp. 78, 79), which must be acknowledged to make the perfect ornament for the Picturesque landscape, needing only the setting of green sward, shady cedar and sulky swans to persuade us that we are all characters out of Thomas Love Peacock, and that everything has been ordained for the best in the best of all possible worlds. When the method is applied in the more abrasive conditions of Islington, as in their Weston Rise housing (pp. 72, 73), we are less convinced of the universality of their vocabulary.

It must be admitted that one of the sources of ambiguity in architecture has nothing directly to do with the particular programmatic intensions of the architect, but rather stems from his often random, sometimes ruthless, commandeering of ready-made forms — those that happen to be available or fashionable at any one time. These are configurations lifted from their original setting and applied with rough justice to the situation as found. The use of recessed pilotis supporting a more or less regular rectangular superstructure is a typical syntagm which has received a wide application and become instantly recognizable. It can be delicate (as it was at Poissy) or powerful (as it was at the Pavillon Suisse). Le Corbusier not only invented this configuration and popularized it, he went on to show how it could be stylistically varied and to explore further attenuations and deformations of it. His design for the monastery of La Tourette, where the stilts of varying height are surmounted by a box which is itself plastically varied, has been a major source of forms for the sixties. The high overhanging storey, as at La Tourette, was taken up by Kallmann, McKinnell and Knowles in their design for Boston City Hall, and it has now become a best-seller. The motive is used, with varied effect, according to the particularity of the programme. It can be a unifying principle, as in the laboratories for the London Zoo by Llewelyn-Davies Weeks Forestier-Walker & Bor (ill. 18); or a reinforcer of the *piano nobile,* as in Michael Brawne's house at Fisher's Pond (ill. 19); or an element of sheer drama, as in Basil Spence's students' union at Southampton University (ill. 20).

In many respects the vocabulary of the sixties has been dominated by elements like this derived from the formal repertoire of Le Corbusier. But whereas earlier borrowings from him were restricted to the period of the international style, they now range over the complete *œuvre* and are applied regardless of the need to preserve a purity of style. Particularly exploited have been his suggestions for varying the configuration of the main mass of cellular accommodation, involving the staggering of successive floors to produce set-backs and overhangs on opposite sides (including the effect of 'high overhang' which we have already noticed). Another variation is produced by turning over the regular mass on to the sloping site, where it can incorporate the hillside in a series of climbing steps. Such forms are capable of rational interpretation: more distinctly emotive in intention has been the use of blank walls and small windows, as at Ronchamp, as the basis of an architecture of expressive blankness. Walls without any windows are protective in nature, whether against bullets or to assist the air-conditioning: insofar as the presence of windows tends to reiterate a purely human scale, their absence allows the shadow of a super-human, or even sub-human, scale to be projected. Trevor Dannatt's school at Bootham (ill. 21) makes a delicate use of expressive blankness, whereas the South Bank Arts Centre makes a rather coarse use of it. Along with the almost inexhaustible repertoire of Corb-derived forms, the sixties saw also a revival of the all-round facade (from Mies) — as used cool in the Economist Building

21

(pp. 181–183) and hot in the Leicester Engineering Building (pp. 116–118); and the impending roof, covered in metal sheeting (mainly from Aalto), as exemplified again in Dannatt's school at Bootham.

Coining new words which will be universally approved is not given to many of us. The language of modern architecture, however it has evolved, is still very largely made up out of money minted by the first generation masters. In any case an architecture which takes seriously its social mission must aim to be widely intelligible, and to do this it must incorporate and reiterate familiar elements if it is to provide recognizable settings for the activities of the community. Thus to the philosophical 'problem of form' is added a political and social dilemma: the architect who sets out to satisfy his client's demand for a distinctive or imposing edifice runs the risk of confusing or alienating the user. The collaboration, sometimes the collusion, of architect and client, in a personal understanding, may just as readily create an obstacle to user enjoyment and participation as facilitate it.

Everything depends on the degree of diffusion of common elements and on their unambiguous application in the majority of cases. It is the work of the 'ordinary' architect which takes on a major importance in creating and answering a norm of expectancy in the user at large. The ordinary architect may have aspirations: is he to keep them in check so as to avoid transmitting them as mere pretensions? If so he runs the risk of perpetrating ghastly good taste. Or is he to fling himself whole-heartedly into the pursuit of the popular image? If so he risks selling out to the merely commercial motivations of the packager and the mass media. It is because no easy solution lies to hand that the design of buildings remains important, and the problem of form a perennial source of interest.

In structuring his solutions, the architect will often be tempted to adopt fashionable sequences which he is not inventing *de novo,* but which may nevertheless be fresh *for him* if he is applying them for the first time. Their derivative status will be forgiven if he works to ensure that their application is rational — that is, not unthinking — in intention. If he takes risks and uses, or arrives at, unfamiliar forms, he must be prepared to be misunderstood. The students' union at Keele University (ill. 22) by Stillman and Eastwick-Field, is far from outrageous in its imagery. Yet it was thought by some of its users to remind them variously of a battleship, a factory, even a gas-chamber. Others, probably a majority, recognized it as a typical institutional facility, bestowing dignity on social events.[38] To the extent that the architect serves one section of the community rather than another, he must accept a disparity in the responses. To the extent that he invents a rhetoric to suit the occasion, he runs the risk of being unintelligible to all. While generally seeking credibility, and avoiding ambiguity, the architect cannot ignore the possibility that deliberate ambiguity may provide a wider credibility.

But ambiguity can also be cultivated. We have seen how the dome of New Hall (ill. 13, 14) was capable of evoking a vague and varied interpretation. Its meaning would have been quite different if it had turned out that it really harboured a six-inch telescope. Lack of specificity in an object permits it to figure more freely in the individual's imagination. A whole school of minimal art, in theatre, in music, and in the plastic arts, has arisen during the sixties to exploit the realization that human perception is highly structured by the internal expectation of the observer, who thus becomes a participant. In

22

26

21. Trevor Dannatt. Assembly hall of Bootham School, York. 1964.
22. Stillman and Eastwick-Field. Students' union building at Keele University. 1962.
23. Sir Basil Spence, Bonnington & Collins. Falmer House, University of Sussex. 1960.

transferring the game of deliberate ambiguity to architecture, Robert Venturi has raised a good deal of controversy,[39] which may be caused more by his practice of it than by the principles themselves. Whether or not we approve of Venturi's game, we do not help to clarify matters if we refuse to recognize that the problem of form exists and is as inescapable as is the problem of self-image for each and every individual. The worst fault in architects is their continuing naïvety, more often hypocrisy, in claiming objective or functional determinism for designs which are patently arbitrary or *retardataire*.

A classic case of the controlled use of ambiguity is that of Denys Lasdun's Royal College of Physicians (pp. 174, 175). This is also a prime example of a building designed to house and symbolize a learned institution. The architect has deliberately divided the symbolic realm into two zones — that of the permanent, and that of the transient. The offices, the lecture hall, the laboratories, are identified as 'transient' by their construction in brick; whereas the ceremonial censor's room and library, and the main staircase hall and dining hall are grouped together in a 'permanent' realm identified by a covering of fine white mosaic. The mosaic is laid on concrete, and its actual physical permanence is marginally less than that of the brickwork, which is also carried on a concrete frame. It is the symbolic content which is relevant. Whether fine mosaic or tough brick better represents the division into permanent and transient is a moot point.[40] Without the architect's script we might not have made the connection.

The ethic of aesthetic

I have tried to show that when we picture architecture as a vehicle for ideas, certain problems of form arise. The form stands between the programme for the building and its content as a cultural object. The architect is concerned with both faces of form, that which refers back to the representation of the programme, and that which refers out to its promulgation. Whatever range of meanings can be read into the final object, they will have a limitation in the empirical facts of the programme, its social purpose, its formulation, and the dialectical process of consultation and adjustment between architect and client by which it is brought to a resolution in a completed building in real time.

This is in itself a complex professional task, and many architects, grappling with it over a five year period of gestation and construction, may be forgiven for wishing to treat it as a professional routine or to automatize it through managerial procedures — any format which relieves them of the necessity of recognizing that they are inescapably participating in the ideological issues of their time.

To begin with, whether or not they wish their product to be examined for content, it *will* be scrutinized by client, critic, and user. Can the architect afford to be indifferent to what they will think? Admittedly, he cannot prevent others from attributing to his building a meaning that suits them, or telling *him* what his intentions were or ought to have been. Erwin Panofksy has pointed out that the symbolic content of an object is virtually infinite; he even accords the unearthing of this content a separate place in art history:

'The discovery and interpretation of these 'symbolic' values (which are often unknown to the artist himself and may even emphatically differ from what he consciously intended to express) is the object of what we may call "iconology" as opposed to "iconography".'[41]

23

Even when we are dealing with an object whose functional purpose is evident, we may still look into it for its symbolic implications, just as we search for functional or representative significance in objects whose purpose is ambiguous. Panofsky continues:

'A spinning machine is perhaps the most impressive manifestation of a functional idea, and an "abstract" painting is perhaps the most expressive manifestation of pure form, but both have a minimum of content.'

Clearly, a building is not necessarily a work of art, nor if it is, does the user have to treat it as one. Whether buildings are high art or utilitarian in concept, they will be used primarily as utilities. But even a simple utility can be imbued with symbolic content, if the users choose to see it so. If, as Meyer claimed, architecture is concerned with order and organization, it will enter into the life experience of men, whether by providing identity and orientation, or just as likely (more likely, if we are to believe the psychologists) by articulating their insecurity or alienation.[42]

Knowing that the material products of his work will become part of the material of life, how should the architect set about his task? He will rarely if ever see himself as doing other than good. (Even Hitler's architect believed in the ideology of his rhetoric.) Knowing that his work will be interpreted for good or ill, should he pay attention to the suggestiveness of his forms? Or should he leave interpretation to others and concentrate on meeting the conditions of the programme as straightforwardly and honestly as possible?

The architect who recognizes the scope of rhetorical persuasion open to him, and who does not doubt his own skill, will seize the opportunity with gusto. Such an architect is Basil Spence. At the University of Sussex (ill. 23) we are astonished at the range and versatility of his acting, playing many parts and varying the characters without budging out of his Falstaffian coat of red brick and dusty concrete. Spence plays to his audience, and by all accounts gets through to them — Sussex is less unpopular than other new universities and his cathedral at Coventry is a box-office success.

An architect who is conscious of the power of his rhetoric, but who employs it with a great deal of restraint, is Denys Lasdun. Like Spence, his vocabulary is in the main derived from Le Corbusier, but this represents only the basis from which he has evolved his own, more limited, more disciplined and more coherent forms. Whereas Spence uses thick and thin, vertical and horizontal elements as he feels like it, Lasdun searches for a consistent and regular expression of the spaces behind the facade. His obsession is with the horizontal — the hovering concrete slab — with its capacity for floating blank walls as if they were weightless. The verticals, on the other hand, are delicate in their distributed form as bearing structure, or are concentrated in the blank masses of the service stacks which penetrate powerfully through the horizontal slabs. The germ of this consistent and extremely controlled style is apparent in the early cluster-block flats of Bethnal Green (ill. 24, 25). It has evolved step by step, until we see it fully deployed at the University of East Anglia (pp. 128, 129). But its most important application will be in the National Theatre (ill. 26) now under construction in London on the South Bank opposite Somerset House.

Another firm of architects who have cultivated a consistent rhetoric of restraint is Yorke Rosenberg Mardall (YRM). We have already noted their part in the translation of SOM to England for Boots. Their method is to look for the simplest building volume or combination of volumes which will satisfy the particularities of the programme, and then to build it to a standard of technical excellence and control. The building will be a loose fit to the functions, rather than display the pressure of functional differentiation on the overall form. The result is usually a building of massive physical presence, the proportion of solid to void carefully organized and the surface controlled at every point. For this purpose they have made white tiles their hallmark — a method of stressing the solid part of the solid-and-void equation with a realistic eye on the English climate. These self-satisfied buildings may irritate the students (at Warwick University): but they are crisp, businesslike and un-fussy. In situations like Gatwick Airport (ill. 27) the rhetoric is exactly right, saying what the building is, and going only a little farther to do this with firmness and elegance.

With James Stirling we come to an architect of quite another kind. His buildings are, if he can manage it, tours de force of technical virtuosity. He pretends to ignore the rhetorical consequences of these heroic gestures, claiming to concentrate whole-heartedly on the particular programme and its translation into a technical entity. Like the Smithsons, he looks rather for a style for the job, and the decision of gravest import is the method of construction to be adopted in each particular case. Each of his buildings

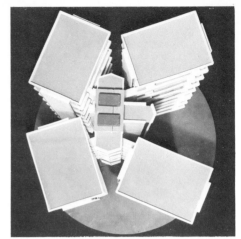

24

25

26

24, 25. Denys Lasdun. Housing at Bethnal Green, London. 1960.
26. Denys Lasdun and Partners. National Theatre, London. Project, revised version. 1969.

27. Yorke Rosenberg Mardall. Gatwick Airport.
1956.
28. Cedric Price. Computer building at London
Airport. 1968.
29. Richard + Su Rogers. Prefabricated house.
1970.
30. Farrell/Grimshaw partnership. Hostel conversion at Paddington. 1967.

27

28

29

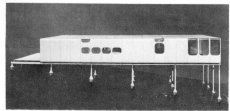

30

29

is a new revelation of his plastic and technical invention. Again we find a basis of Corbusier in the elements but also traces of Wright and the Constructivists. The amalgam is a personal one, and expresses a narrowly concentrated vision and will power. As such, he has already become a source-book, and his use of stepped greenhouse glass is now a cliché for others.

Finally, with Cedric Price, we come to an architect who denies a rhetorical intention. For him, the building should be no more than an enabler, a mechanism for allowing the things you want to happen, to happen. In this he follows Hannes Meyer at his purest. The aviary at London Zoo (pp. 168, 169) is highly determined — by the conditions for viewing the birds and for the demonstration of their several habitats, as much as by the *parti* of a suspended tensegrity structure. In the computer building at London Airport (ill. 28) we find the architect equally determined to efface himself. This is a facility, like a computer or a filing cabinet, not to be confused with any pathetic fallacy. The basis of this design is the Price slogan — well serviced anonymity. We may be forgiven, however, for seeing in the careful positioning of the entrance and its ramp, and the angled rainwater pipes, an attention to detail which betrays the trained eye at work. This subdued and almost subfusc building is a little like the bowler hat of René Magritte: it is a gleam in someone's eye.

Among the younger architects who have already made some mark on the sixties are Norman Forster and Richard Rogers (separately now, formerly together, with spouses, as Team 4). Terence Farrell and Nicholas Grimshaw, and Edward Cullinan. They offer an interesting variety of approach. Foster and Rogers, with different degrees of emphasis, are pushing architecture closer to industrial design. Foster's interest is in identifying a strategy which will serve his client's goals (ill. 29; pp. 190–193), whether or not a permanent building will result from this. Rogers is more keyed to the building as an assembly of high-technology components (ill. 30, 31) which will be immaculate in their manufacture and style. In both cases the rhetoric is concerned more with the status of the object than with articulating a realm of public values. With Farrell and Grimshaw we have an energetic team, alert to ways and means of meeting the exigencies of each job as it comes. In the bathroom tower behind Westbourne Terrace in Paddington (ill. 32, 33) they pioneered the production of plastic sanitary units. But their design needs to be understood as a total response to a problem of converting old houses cheaply into students' hostels. The bathroom tower is spectacular, as an addition. What is equally ingenious is the concentration of new services outside the old structure, leaving only the simple subdivision of rooms in the old technology of block and plaster to be managed internally. This is a 'hot' solution. In their flats at Regents Park they show that they can play it cool too.

Edward Cullinan is a young architect with a warm heart and a cool head. More than any other, he has shown an intention to remake the symbolic content of shelter. He is perfectly conversant with the range of technology available, but gives a prime place to the expressive content of the wall and the roof. He aims not at rhetoric, but at pure poetry.

In these examples of some of the new figures arriving on the scene, we may begin to discern the shape of the seventies. They appear to presage a fresh approach to the problem of form, largely by ignoring it. They are confident in the ethic of aesthetic.

In retrospect the sixties appear to represent an uneasy period of formalism, in which the functionalist basis of design is questioned, and a self-conscious eye turned on the effect of form. The conflict between social duty and the expressive content of built form has been acutely felt. Yet the realization that pure objectivity in translating the building task into built form is philosophically impossible has not lessened the emotional hunger for objectivity, whether rational or ritual in nature. During the sixties many architects appear to have operated in a state of schizophrenia, unable to accept the formal consequences of their decisions, yet unable to achieve even a consensus objectively without recourse to the representational nature of forms.

Perhaps it is inevitable, in such circumstances, that the concepts of ethic and aesthetic should be confused. Ethic is offered as aesthetic, and aesthetic as ethic. In the ethical fifties, the CLASP system was at its inception a purely rational means of meeting a building task: but in 1960 a CLASP school took the palm of the Milan Triennale — a recognition of its elegance as well as its rationality.

The Brutalist sixties which on the whole represent a descent into aesthetic formalism were nevertheless initially the result of a genuine impulse to throw off ritualized convention and penetrate to the essentials of life. In this process, a part at least of the transfer of values is due to the dialectic of history with its inevitable toll in entropy. But another part of it is due to the continual fluctuation of ideology between ethic and aesthetic. What originates as ethic turns out be aesthetic. It was the ethical content in the origin of Brutalism which gave it its moral appeal. What aesthetic does is to articulate for us our ideology. It is paradoxical that the ethic should turn out to be more promise than performance, but there is a reason for this: to transform the ethic of society is the work of a generation of least. The forces resisting change are dispersed through the fabric of society, where they have become set and ritualized. The forces for change are bonded together and impatient. It is inevitable that they should seize on what can be modified and project an image of an alternative, a better state of affairs. Aesthetic is the means at hand of doing this. At one and the same time it portrays a viable alternative in convincing detail, and identifies it as a banner for a new way of life. By modifying the life-style, it dissolves the inevitability of the accepted rituals, and makes way for social change.

Notes

1 'Canons of Criticism: A conversation between Berthold Lubetkin and Lionel Brett', *The Architectural Review*, March 1951.

2 In *The Architectural Review*, April 1954.

3 *Ibid.*

4 *Op. cit.* ('Canons of Criticism').

5 A phrase invented by *The Architectural Review*, along with the New Humanism and the New Eclecticism. As the chief organ of architectural theory, the *Review* was watching closely for the emergence of new movements in architecture.

6 The phrase was invented by Stendhal to describe English manners and morals in *De l'amour* (1822). See Robert Maxwell, 'Sweet Disorder and the Carefully Careless', *Architectural Design*, April 1971.

7 Alison and Peter Smithson in *The Architectural Review,* April 1954.

8 Reyner Banham, *The New Brutalism*, 1966.

9 From the architects' specification: 'The Contractor should aim at a high standard of basic construction, as in a small warehouse.'

10 Colin Rowe, in a series of articles published in *The Architectural Review* in the late forties, had been among the first to compare Le Corbusier with Palladio, and hence to imply that modern architecture was not of a different nature to the architecture of classic times. In so doing, he brought to the attention of practising architects a historical perspective first mooted by Emil Kaufmann in 1933.

11 Banham, *op. cit.*

12 Both Colin Rowe and Martin Myerson, from very different points of view, have suggested that the Economist Building is the perfect example of the English establishment at work.

13 Among English architects directly influenced by the Smithsons are John Killick, Bill Howell, Sandy Wilson, Alan Colquhoun, John Voelcker, James Gowan, Christopher Dean, Warren Chalk and Ron Herron.

14 In a letter to K. Tiege, written in 1929, published as 'Defense de l'Architecture' in *L'Architecture d'Aujourd'hui*, 10 (1933). I am indebted to Alan Colquhoun for his English translation of this interesting document, now in preparation.

15 Claude Schnaidt, *Hannes Meyer*, 1965.

16 *Ibid.*

17 *Ibid.*

18 I am referring to Saussure's concepts of *langue* and *parole* in his analysis of language.

19 Kenneth Frampton, 'The humanist v. the utilitarian ideal', *Architectural Design*, March 1968.

20 Schnaidt, *op. cit.*

21 A semiological theory of architecture, and of non-verbal systems of signs, has so far only been sketched in by Roland Barthes: see *Elements of Semiology*, 1967.

22 Le Corbusier, letter to K. Tiege (see note 14).

23 Ernst Cassirer, *The Philosophy of Symbolic Forms*, 1957.

24 'Saussure imagines that at the (entirely theoretical) origin of meaning, ideas and sounds form two floating, labile, continuous and parallel masses of substances; meaning intervenes when one cuts at the same time and at a single stroke into these two masses. The signs thus produced are therefore *articuli*; meaning is therefore an order with chaos on either side, but this order is essentially a division. The language is an intermediate object between sound and thought.' Barthes, *op. cit.*

25 See Jürgen Joedicke, *Architecture since 1945: Sources and Directions*, 1969: 'As the inherent engagement of modern architecture with function and structure has lapsed, the legitimate and necessary search for novelty leads to a search for novelty at any price.'

26 Frank Jenkins, *Architect and Patron*, 1961.

27 *Ibid.*

28 There is about one doctor for every 750 people.

29 In the United States, the comparable figure five years ago had sunk to only 14%.

30 Barthes, *op. cit.*

31 Reyner Banham, *Theory and Design in the First Machine Age*, 1960.

32 *Ibid.*

33 Peter Smithson, 'Without rhetoric', *Architectural Design*, January 1967.

34 Alison Smithson (ed.) 'Team 10 Primer', *Architectural Design*, December 1962.

35 Amédée Ozenfant, *Foundations of Modern Art*, 1931.

36 Ada Louise Huxtable, reviewing the Venturi show in New York, in October 1971, said that his arguments had 'split the profession down the middle, 90% against'.

37 See *Architectural Design*, December 1971.

38 See Conrad Jameson in *The Architects' Journal*, 27 October 1971.

39 Robert Venturi, *Complexity and Contradiction in Architecture*, 1966.

40 See the author's critical discussion of this building in *The Architectural Review*, April 1965.

41 Erwin Panofsky, *Meaning in the Visual Arts*, 1955.

42 Research carried out by a team of industrial psychologists has suggested that bad conditions of work are criticized more than good conditions are praised. Bad conditions appear to symbolize insecurity more readily than good conditions symbolize success. See Herzberg et al., *The Motivation to Work*, 1959.

John Winter and Associates
Two houses in Belsize Park, London, 1969

The building owner built two houses, one for himself and his family to live in, one for sale to help reduce the cost of the operation. The houses are set back from each other and have their entrances on opposite sides for increased privacy. The owner's house has three storeys, with kitchen, dining area, and family room on the ground level, children's rooms on the first floor, and living room and master bedroom in the top storey. The smaller two-storeyed house is organized in the customary way, with kitchen, dining area and living room on the ground level, and bedrooms in the upper storey. The construction is of light-weight concrete blocks, faced externally with white mosaic. The structural cross walls follow a uniform 3 m. (9 ft. 10 in.) bay system so that all floor joints are identical. Windows are all of a standard dimension, and are double-glazed in aluminium frames.

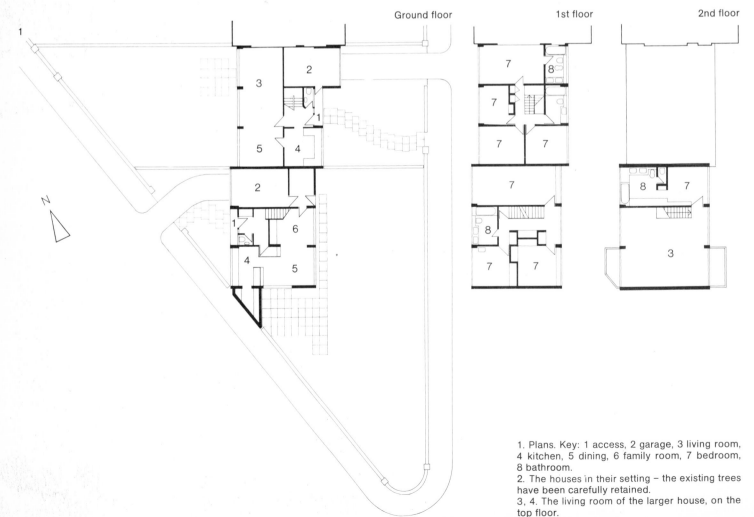

Ground floor   1st floor   2nd floor

1. Plans. Key: 1 access, 2 garage, 3 living room, 4 kitchen, 5 dining, 6 family room, 7 bedroom, 8 bathroom.
2. The houses in their setting – the existing trees have been carefully retained.
3, 4. The living room of the larger house, on the top floor.

2

3

4

James Gowan
Schreiber house, Hampstead, London, 1963

This house was designed for an industrialist who specializes in wood-engineering. The house and its equipment have been treated as an integrated system. It is planned on four levels — service rooms in the basement, living rooms on the ground floor, the main bedrooms on the first floor and children's rooms and studio on the second floor. Each floor is arranged as an open suite, but there are double doors at strategic points which can be folded into position to isolate individual rooms when privacy is required. The house is built of brick cross walls organized on a quadrangular unit dimension of 0.90 m. (3 ft.). The modular nature of the spaces is made evident by the wall panelling, which follows the same grid.
In contrast, the swimming pool, added later by the same architect, follows the determining form of a circle.

1

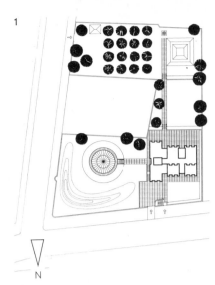

N

2

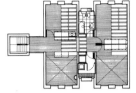

2nd floor

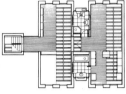

1st floor

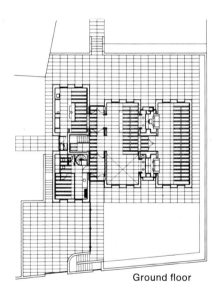

Ground floor

1. Site layout:
2. The house seen from the street.
3. Plans of the house.
4. The house seen from the garden.
5. Section through the house, and (left and right)
details of the structure.

Basement

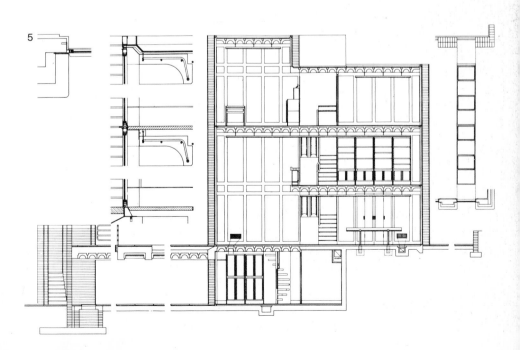

6. Living room.
7. Kitchen and dining room.
8. Plan and section of the swimming pool.
9. The swimming pool seen from the house.
10. Coloured bands emphasize the shape of the pool.

9

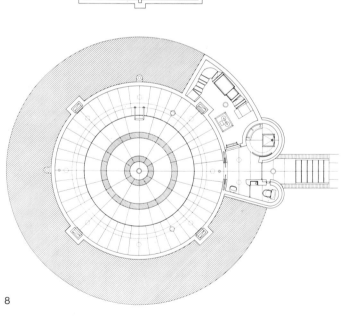

8

10

Colin St John Wilson
Two houses in Cambridge, 1963

The two houses were designed and built together, in a form capable of giving rise to continuous terraces, but with considerable variety of accommodation for each dwelling. Both privacy and orientation to sunlight are achieved by grouping the living accommodation around a paved patio.

The architect's own house is entered between open piers supporting a studio, thence into a small courtyard paved with white gravel. The living room is double height, with a library in the gallery overlooking the main space.

The walls are constructed of white concrete blocks, the ceilings of white aggregate concrete. Exposed wood is treated with preservative. Floors are white rubber tiles, with electric underfloor heating panels. The use of partly absorbent blocks has created a pleasant quality of suffused light.

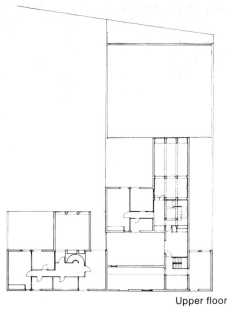

Upper floor

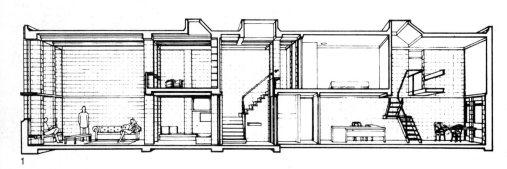

1

2

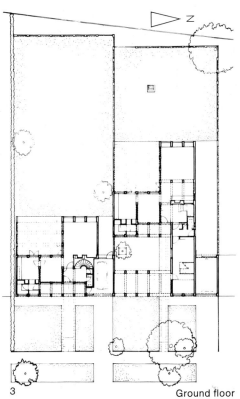

3

Ground floor

38

4

1. Section through the architect's house.
2. The architect's house seen from the garden. Sculpture by Paolozzi.
3. Plans.
4. The architect's house seen from the street. The piers in front support the studio.
5, 6. Living room of the architect's house.

5

6

Colin St John Wilson with Mary Jane Long
Cornford house, Cambridge, 1966

The client required a house for himself, his wife, and two sons who visit only occasionally. He was quite specific about the work requirements — a painter's studio for himself, a library for his wife — and also about the main areas of relaxation.

The form of the house is a response to these intentions, and is well suited to the topography of the site, where the only significant prospect lies due south, precisely on the diagonal of the building plot.

The double-height space of the living room forms the centre of the structure, with a spatial concentration on the hearth, and an opening out to the sun, the view, and the garden terrace on the diagonal.

The structure is based on a module of 1.8 m. (5 ft. 11 in.). The monopitch timber roof trusses rest on round timber columns defining the living space and the garden terrace, thus linking the inward and outward aspects of the house. The columnar structure, most of the interior partitions and the first floor ceiling are all of natural timber. Central heating is provided by a gas-fired warm air system.

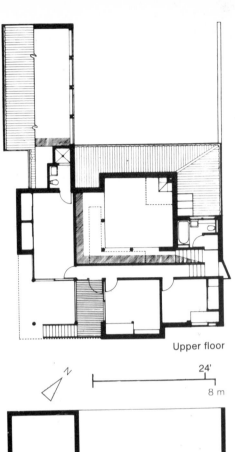

Upper floor

24'

8 m

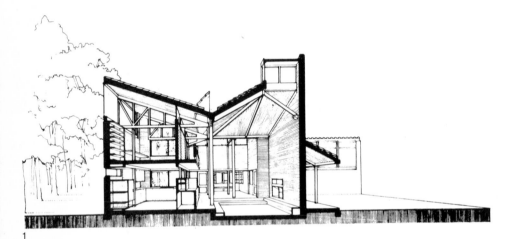

1

2

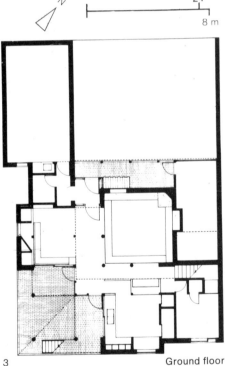

3

Ground floor

40

4

5

1. Section.
2. The house seen from the south.
3. Plans.
4. The house seen from the north-east.
5. The entrance court, with studio on the right.
6. The bedroom gallery seen from the staircase.
7. Detail of structure in the living room.

6

41

7

Barry Gasson and John Meunier
Wendon house, Barton, near Cambridge, 1965

This house was designed for a family who wanted something different from the conventional suburban villa, where the living room is just another box and the staircase a necessary chore. The architects have dramatized the relationship between the individual members of the family and the shared family scene, by winding the private rooms around the main living space on a continuous square ramp. The living room takes on something of the character of an exhibition hall, or of a theatre, a little larger than life.
The construction is of white aggregate concrete block walls with timber floors. The spiralling rooms and the central space are structurally distinct, with the ramp occupying the gap. Double glazing and an insulated cavity in the walls permit an economical and flexible electrical heating system by means of concealed ceiling panels.

1

2

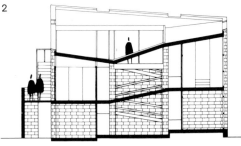

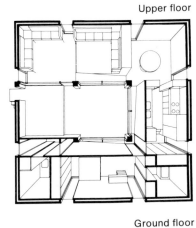

Upper floor

Ground floor

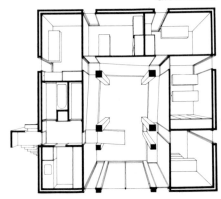

1. The house seen from the street.
2. Plans and section.
3. Axonometric view.
4. The first floor entrance with a glimpse of the roof terrace.
5. The central living room with the wrap-round ramp.

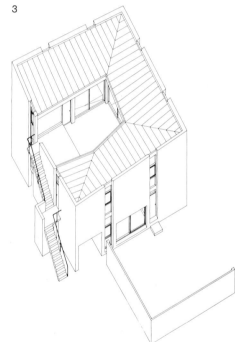

Michael Brawne
The architect's own house in Hampstead, London, 1959

The architect designed this house for his own family. It occupies a narrow plot in a built-up street and is intended to be unmistakably a town house.

A very careful use has been made of a restricted volume. The middle floor of the three is level with the rear garden and acts as the living room, with the kitchen installed on a raised platform like a bar, so as not to interrupt the space. The lowest level has the parents' bedroom suite, the top level has the children's rooms. A tiny balcony at the end of the upper landing, and sensitive placing of windows at the top of the staircase void, create a remarkable sense of spaciousness in so small a house.

Simple materials — brick and timber — have been used and displayed as a foil to the transitory clutter of family life. The kitchen fitments have been designed on ergonomic principles to be as labour-saving as possible.

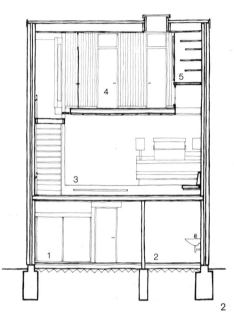

1. The house seen from the garden. The bridge in the foreground connects the first floor with the garden.
2. Section. Key: 1 dressing room, 2 bathroom, 3 dining area, 4 corridor, 5 cupboard.

44

3

3. View down the staircase void. The internal window projects from one of the children's bedrooms.
4. Plans. Key: 1 steps from the pavement to the raised ground floor, 2 dustbin enclosure, 3 entrance, 4 store, 5 adult's bedroom, 6 bathroom, 7 dressing room, 8 kitchen, 9 dining, 10 sitting, 11 bridge to the garden, 12 children's room.
5. The dining area.
6. The living room seen from the bridge.

5

4

2nd floor

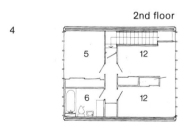

1st floor

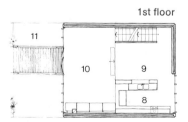

Ground floor

6

Stout & Litchfield
Weekend house at Shipton-under-Wychwood, Gloucestershire, 1962

A weekend house in the Cotswolds constructed of indigenous materials, this design
was originally refused planning permission by the local planning authority as aesthet-
ically unsuitable. Consent was eventually granted only after a public inquiry.
It is true that although made of local materials, the final character of the house is that
of a sophisticated object. Each room has a separate expression and a different roof
shape, so that the house appears as a cluster of cubic volumes, their profiles dramatically
juxtaposed; carefully careless rather than randomly disordered, exotic and Mediterranean rather than native and northern.
The stone walls carry stone tile roofs on pine rafters. The floors are tiled, with underfloor
electric heating.

1

1. The house seen from the north.
2. Plan and section. Key: 1 entrance, 2 bedroom, 3 kitchen and dining area, 4 living room, 5 covered passage, 6 patio, 7 covered sitting area, 8 store room.
3. The water garden.
4. Kitchen and dining area.

3

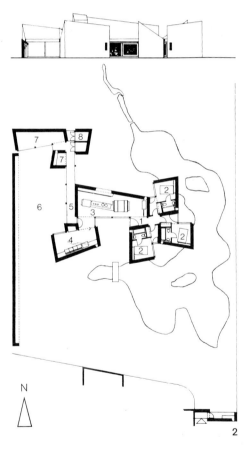

N

2

4

Brett and Pollen
Tower house at Christmas Common, Oxfordshire, 1967

This house was built on extensive parkland for Lionel Brett (Viscount Esher) himself.
It rises as a tower amongst the tall trees partly to combat their immense scale and
partly to capture sunlight at all times of the day. A swimming pool has been excavated
beside the house, so close that it partly surrounds it like a moat. A turret on the east
face contains a passenger lift.
Compact and rather massive, the house could easily be taken for a converted mill:
its forms are reminiscent of the eighteenth-century functional building beloved of *The
Architectural Review.*
It is constructed of load-bearing brown bricks with a slab roof. The large windows
are double-glazed. Heating is by ducted warm air. The winter heating system is switched
in summer to heat the pool.

2

3rd floor

2nd floor

1st floor

Ground floor

Basement

3

4

1. The house seen from the west.
2. Plans. Key: 1 garage, 2 kitchen, 3 dining, 4 store room, 5 play, 6 study, 7 living room, 8 bedroom, 9 bathroom.
3. The house seen from the south. The living room has a projecting concrete balcony; below, a dining terrace near the swimming pool.
4. Kitchen and dining area.

1

2

3

Richard + Su Rogers
House at Creek Vean, Cornwall, 1966

This house is built on a steep slope overlooking a small river. It had to be integrated into the sloping ground, while taking advantage of the sun and view. The client wished also to house a collection of modern paintings and sculpture.

The structure is organized in two sections. The first, on two levels, contains the living room with entrance hall, and stairs down to dining-kitchen, and hence to the second section which contains study and bedrooms. The two sections are separated by an entrance terrace, approached by a bridge, and leading down to the waterside. The transverse axis at the lower level is a picture gallery and also leads to the other rooms. The arrangement gives a very open access to the upper level, while allowing greater privacy to the lower one.

The house walls are constructed of honey-coloured concrete blocks, with concrete floors on permanent plywood forms. Heating is by an oil-fired system with hot air ducted over the structured ceilings.

5

6

7

1. General view from the river.
2. Site layout.
3. The entrance approached by a bridge.
4. View from the north.
5. The gallery leading north, with the study to the left.
6. The gallery leading south, with the kitchen below.
7. The dining-kitchen.
8. Plans.

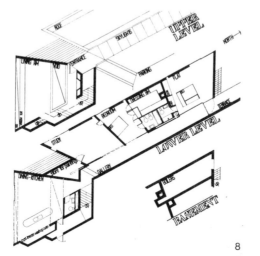

8

N. Foster, W. Foster, R. Rogers
House in Radlett, Hertfordshire, 1967

This house, situated in suburban country north of London, occupies a long narrow site sloping north towards the view. In order to have sunlight while taking advantage of the views to the north, the house has been planned with a single storey arranged as a series of platforms stepping down the slope. At each change in level rooflights admit the sun.
Cross walls divide the house into three zones, two of which can be opened to each other by sliding screens. The third has the bedrooms. Additional rooms can be added, if required.

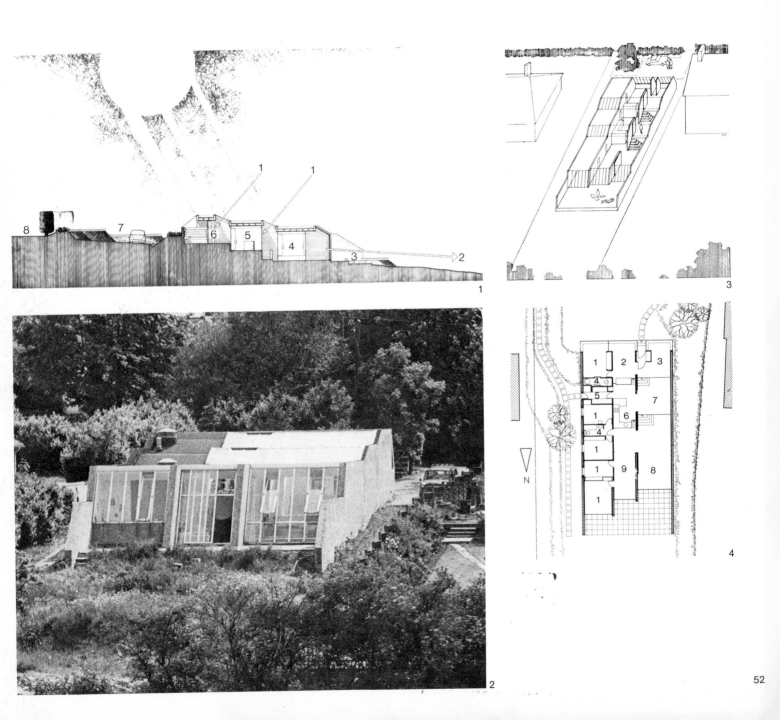

1

3

2

4

52

5

53

1. Section. Key: 1 indirect north light, 2 view, 3 terrace, 4 living room, 5 dining room, 6 study, 7 forecourt, 8 road.
2. The house seen from the garden. The sloping glass walls reduce the overshadowing on this north face.
3. Axonometric view.
4. Plan. Key: 1 bedroom, 2 conservatory, 3 study, 4 bathroom, 5 utility, 6 kitchen, 7 dining room, 8 living room, 9 playroom.
5. The main living spaces seen from the south.

Phippen/Randall and Parkes
The Ryde, Hatfield New Town, 1964

This development by a private housing association makes use of left-over land between the official residential zone and a pocket of industrial land adjoining a railway. The industry, a corn mill, is a source of both visual and aural disturbance. The architects chose a narrow frontage layout, with single-storey houses, as a means of creating adequate visual and aural privacy, and of fitting in sufficient units to make the venture feasible for householders with modest resources. Rather than open to the view, the houses open to the sky, with internal courts and roof lights. A surprising sense of light and spaciousness results. A club, children's playground and tennis court are included on the private side. Each house has an adjacent garage.

The construction is of single timber beams spanning between cross walls, with a central timber beam supported on posts. This structural form allows considerable flexibility in future adaptation of the internal layout. In the plans as built, some variation of use of the rooms has already been catered for. Background temperatures are maintained by underfloor electrical heating panels.

1

2
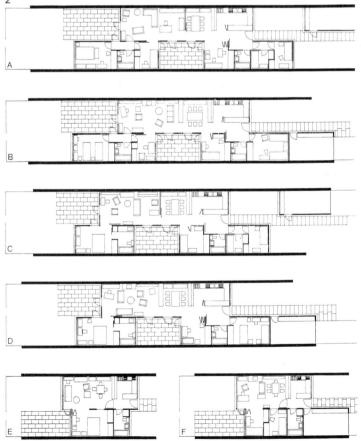

54

3

4

1. Aerial view.
2. Variations in house layout and size.
3. One of the larger houses seen from the garden.
4. View from the street.

5

6

7

8

5. Patio.
6. Garden.
7. Living room and patio.
8. Dining room and kitchen.

Phippen/Randall and Parkes
Houses in Turnpike Place, Crawley New Town, 1968

This is another example of the skilful utilization of left-over land, and of the layout of houses in compact arrangements which had formerly been thought suitable only for blocks of flats. In this case, two-storey houses are combined with a three-storey block containing two duplex apartments. Careful placing of windows and roof lights enables the two-storey houses to be placed very close together, separated only by a narrow pedestrian access passage.
Traditional brick construction is used both for economy and to provide adequate standards of sound insulation.

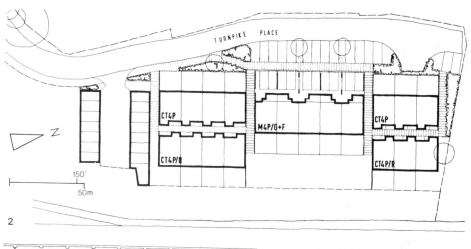

1. Access passage between two CT4P blocks.
2. Site layout.
3, 4. Plans.

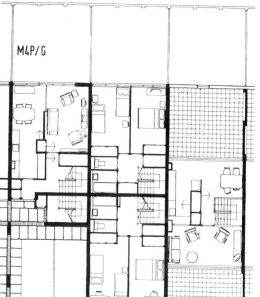

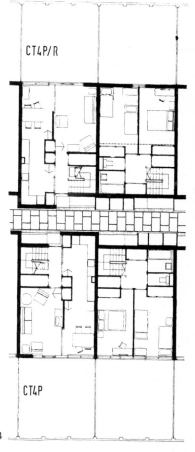

5

M4P/F

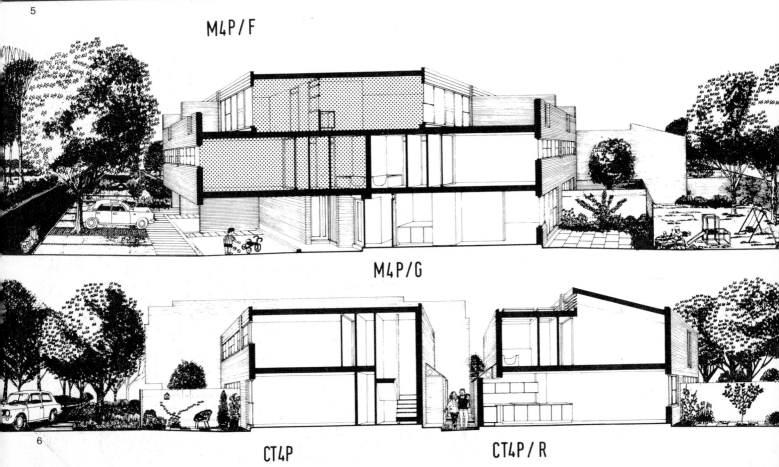

M4P/G

CT4P   CT4P/R

6

7

5. The complex seen from the south-west. Garages in the front.
6. Perspective section.
7. Entrance area in block M4P.
8. Kitchen in block M4P.
9. Block M4P seen from the south-west.

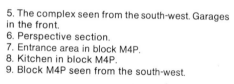

9

Neylan and Ungless
Housing in Linden Grove, London, 1967

In this scheme, a pedestrian access passage is again used as the organizing principle for another close-knit housing layout. The passage changes in level with the ground and also varies in width, widening into a small square at one end and contracting at the other end into a partially roofed arcade, the houses running together to form bridges. Only the front doors open to the access passage: the houses face away towards private terraces or gardens on the periphery of the site which is screened by trees and planting. A group of houses for old people, however, has windows opening to the access space. Wheeled traffic is segregated to one side of the site.
The construction is again of traditional materials, comprising brick cross walls, brick or slate covered walls and timber or concrete floors.

1

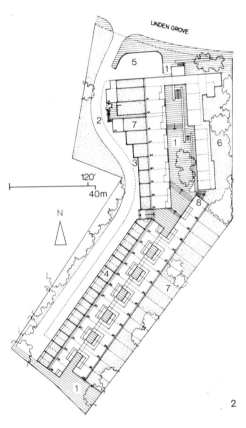

2

1. The narrow passage at the south end, with the upper level of the houses linking to form bridges.
2. Site layout. Key: 1 pedestrian walk, 2 road, 3 hard standing, 4 garages with terrace gardens above, 5 parking area, 6 old people's garden, 7 private gardens, 8 laundry.
3. Plans of a two-house unit at the south end. Key: 1 pedestrian walk, 2 entry, 3 store, 4 living room, 5 kitchen, 6 dining, 7 bedroom.
4. The private terrace of a house at the south end.
5. Steps leading from the access road at the mid-point of the layout.

3

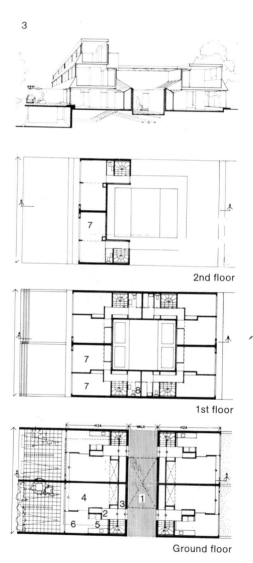

2nd floor

1st floor

Ground floor

4

5

Neylan and Ungless
Bishopsfield and Charters Cross, Harlow, 1963

The architects have stated very clearly that their intention in this design was to group individual houses together to form a whole which from outside is a recognizable and definite place and from inside has an immediately comprehensible structure. Other aims were the segregation of wheeled traffic and a high degree of privacy for each household.
These ends have been achieved by creating a covered parking, garage and service area for vehicles, the roof of which is a pedestrian piazza. Around the piazza is a ring of flats and maisonettes, and outside this ring an outer ring of courtyard houses accessible from pedestrian lanes running down the slope as in Mediterranean hill-towns. Construction is of brick cross walls and external walls with concrete floors and timber roofs.

1

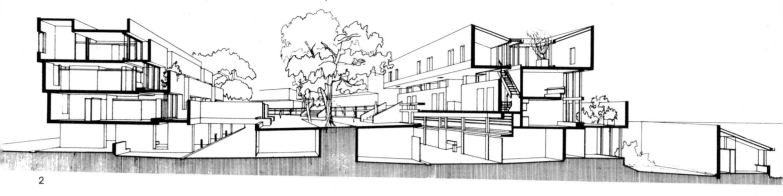

2

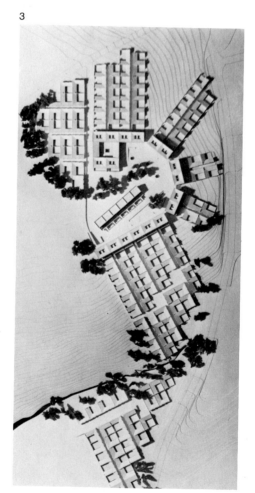

3

4

5

1. The ring around the central piazza.
2. Perspective section through part of the piazza.
3. Model of site layout.
4. The piazza.
5. Terraced houses on the piazza (on the left in the section).

6. Perspective section through living room of a courtyard house.
7, 8, 9. Pedestrian areas between courtyard houses.

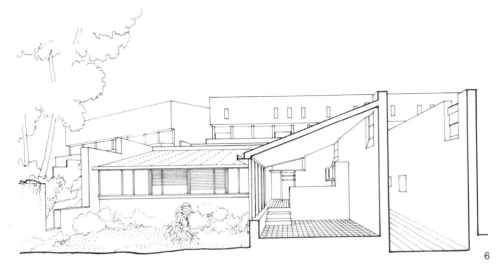

6

7

9

8

Chamberlin, Powell & Bon
Vanbrugh Park, Greenwich, 1962

This scheme was commissioned by a public client — the Borough of Greenwich. The Borough Council wanted a mixture of houses and flats. The majority of the flats have been concentrated in one eight-storey block at the north end of the site, exploiting the view north towards the Thames estuary. A few flats have been arranged as single-storey dwellings built over garages. The greater part of the site is organized with two-storey blocks forming courts, and although an access road cuts through the middle of the layout, it is quiet and combines with the squares and walkways to provide an environment favouring the pedestrian. The main walkway penetrates the apartment block as if to underline the importance of the pedestrian system.
The concrete blocks of which the houses have been constructed are painted, to comply with building regulations; the concrete frame of the apartment block has been stained to mask weathering patterns. The houses have solid-fuel stoves incorporated into a massive heatsink designed as part of the staircase.

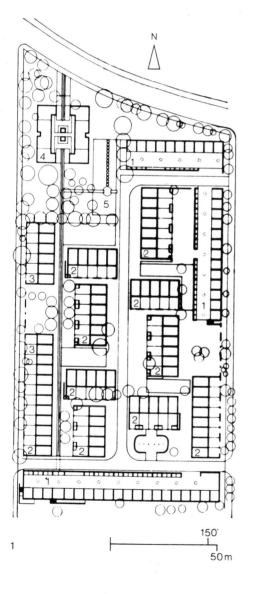

150'
50m

1

2

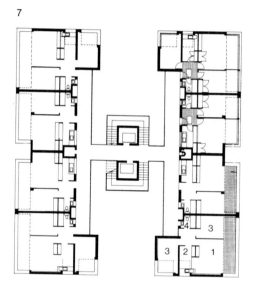

3. Pool.
4. Pedestrian walkway.
5. Living room in a row house.
6. Living room in a mews flat.
7. Plan of a typical floor in the tower block. Key:
1 living room, 2 kitchen, 3 bedroom, 4 bathroom.
8. The tower block seen from the south.
9. The main pedestrian walkway, with the tower block in the background.

1

1. The tower seen from the adjoining railway land.
2. Main room of a penthouse.
3. Plans. Key: 1 living room, 2 bedroom, 3 kitchen, 4 study, 5 ducts, 6 sunken bath, 7 void, 8 lift motor room.
4. Living room of a typical flat.

Farrell/Grimshaw Partnership
125 Park Road, Regents Park, London, 1968

This substantial block of flats was financed by a co-ownership society (Mercury Housing Society Ltd), showing that this method of development is as feasible in central areas as is the low-cost low-rise development in suburban or new town situations. Nevertheless, costs of construction had to be carefully controlled, and to achieve this while leaving a satisfactory level of free choice to the prospective tenants, the architects were led to a cool and neutral solution, suggestive more of an office block than of a block of flats. Between the central structural core and the uniformly fenestrated skin lies a completely undifferentiated ring of floor space, capable of subdivision to suit individual tenants in many varied ways, some of which are illustrated. To achieve this while satisfying the building regulations was itself a major part of the building task. The structure consists of a reinforced concrete core tower and round columns following the perimeter, on piled foundations. The cladding and windows are secured in such a manner that the windows are free from structural mullions. The external cladding is of corrugated aluminium sheets.

2

68

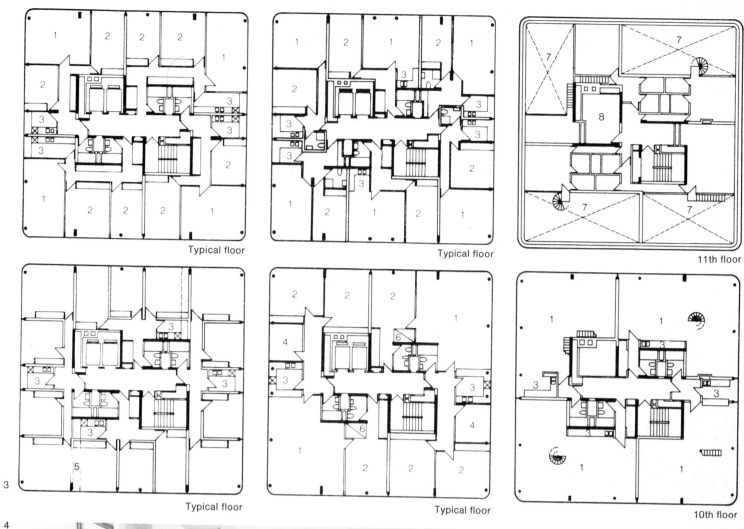

Typical floor

Typical floor

11th floor

3

Typical floor

Typical floor

10th floor

4

Patrick Hodgkinson, with Sir Leslie Martin
Foundling Estate Development, Bloomsbury, London, 1968

This is an *unité d'habitation* in which a number of related functions — shops, restaurants, a cinema, some professional offices, and so on, are incorporated.
The housing is arranged as a double bank of flats on the long sides of a large rectangle. Garaging for cars and parking for shops occupies the podium, with the main commercial facilities grouped along the central axis. The roof of the garage and shopping podium forms a public terrace.
All the living rooms include a glazed 'winter garden' forming an enclosed part of the balcony projections. With the raking of the building volume, this permits sunlight to enter living rooms for a long part of each day.
Construction is in reinforced concrete, with precast concrete facing panels.

1

2

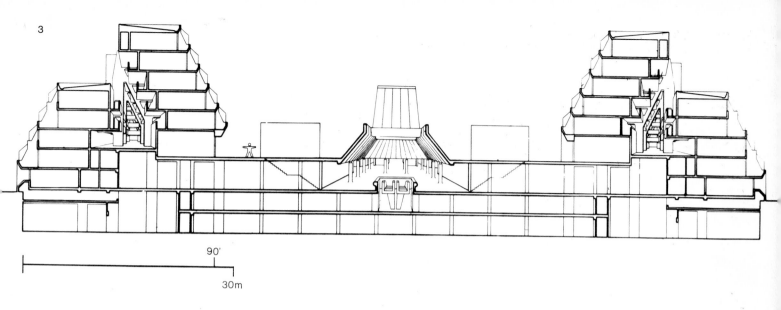

3

90'

30m

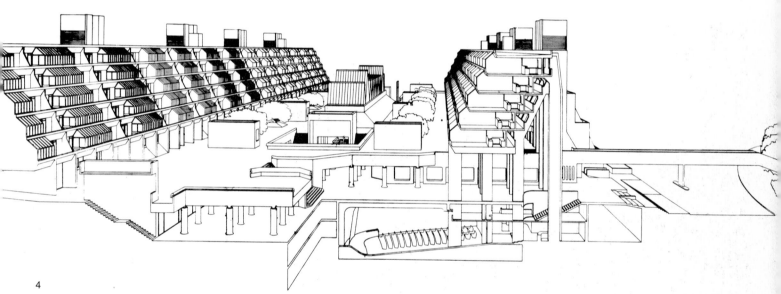

4

5

1, 2. General views.
3. Cross section through the complex.
4. Axonometric view of the total complex.
5. Axonometric view of a flat.

Howell, Killick, Partridge and Amis
Weston Rise Housing Estate, Islington, London, 1965

This housing was carried out for the Greater London Council which required a high density development with a full range of family dwellings but a higher than usual proportion of one and two room flats for old people. The architects decided to use narrow-frontage scissor-type maisonettes in combination with gallery-access flats. The latter back on to the noisier main road to the north, while the two-way looking maisonettes are related to the quieter road on the west of the site. Raised terraces for the older people look out towards the south over the main space of the site which contains a children's playspace arranged on the roof of a parking garage.

The development is divided into five blocks, segregated by access towers. As the ground level rises steeply to the north the blocks vary in height from ten to six storeys, but the roof line is level throughout.

Construction is of *in situ* concrete floors carried on structural brick cross walls. The heavy precast face units provide a consistent appearance to the varying room dispositions, whether living rooms, bedrooms, balconies or access galleries. The service towers are of *in situ* concrete with board marks exposed.

1. Detail of the elevation system.
2. Site layout.
3. The complex seen from the south.

1

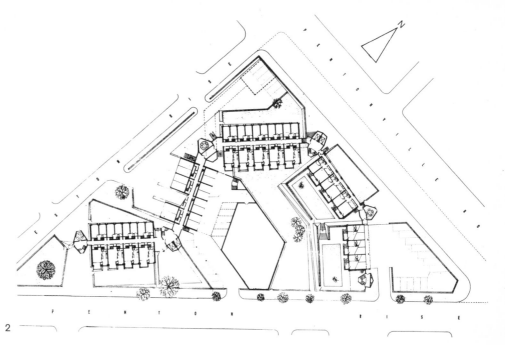

2

3

Greater London Council, Department of Architecture and Civic Design
Thamesmead Development, Woolwich-Erith, London, Phase 1, 1966

Thamesmead is the equivalent of a new town to house 60,000 people, but is unusual in being built not only within the area of Greater London, but on the banks of the Thames. This is made possible through the reclamation of derelict land and marsh. It has been designed as a balanced community, with a high average density, and good transport links. The riverside situation has been exploited by creating a network of lakes, canals and open spaces.

In the phase 1 development we find a combination of thirteen-storey point blocks, linear housing with maisonettes arranged along a pedestrian spine, and three-storey housing arranged in squares. Communal facilities include schools, shopping and medical centres, and a district heating plant.

2

1

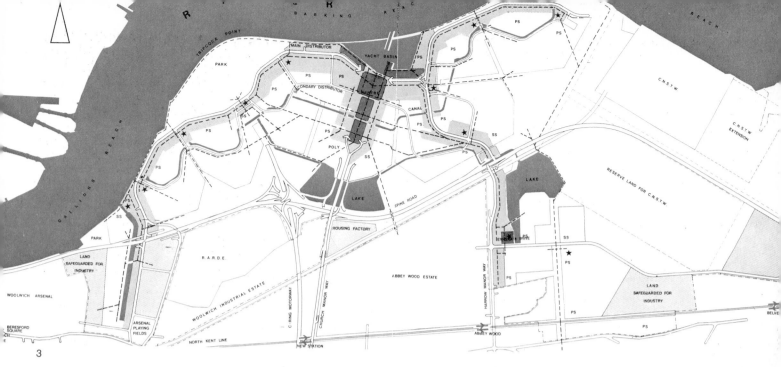

3

4

1. Model of the complete development. Phase 1
is grouped around the artificial lake towards the
centre of the picture.
2. Model of phase 1.
3. General plan of Thamesmead.
4. The terrace houses on the western lake shore;
two maisonettes above parking garages.

A

C

D

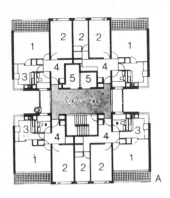

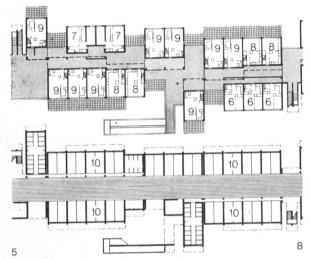

5

B

6

7

5. Plans. Key: A point block, B terrace houses, C row house with two storeys, D row house with three storeys; 1 living room, 2 bedroom, 3 kitchen, 4 entry, 5 lift, 6 one-room apartment, 7 two-room apartment, 8 small maisonette, 9 large maisonette, 10 garages.
6. The terrace houses on the lake shore seen from the west.
7. Centre of phase 1.

Howell, Killick, Partridge and Amis
St Anne's College, Oxford, 1962

The Wolfson and Rayne buildings, together with the new gatehouse, are the completed sections of a development plan for St Anne's College which was prepared in 1960. Although changes have been made in the plan during these years, the main conception of a sweeping line of six linked and curved blocks has remained valid.

The two dormitory blocks contain study-bedrooms for undergraduate students, two suites for fellows and a few larger rooms for graduates or senior students. A lobby containing washbasin, wardrobe and storage cupboards insulates the individual study from the corridor and this service zone can be screened off by a sliding door. The side walls of each room radiate at 4°, and this generates a curved building with highly modelled convex sides and angled end walls, while the internal corridor and communal services expand to accommodate a generous spiral stair in the centre.

The construction is of reinforced concrete, and embodies the use of room size splayed box-frames, which in this case provide small balconies for each room. The small scale and decorative effect of the construction successfully offset the use of raw materials.

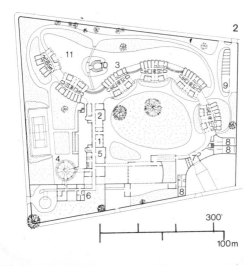

300'

100m   78

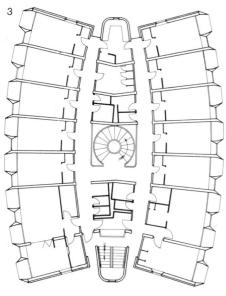

1. The two complete blocks: Wolfson (left) and Rayne (right).
2. Site layout. Key: 1 senior common room, 2 junior common room, 3 dormitory blocks, 4 new library and teaching block, 5 teaching space, 6 principal's house, 7 gatehouse, 8 service room, 9 garages and bicycle stands, 10 music room, 11 lake.
3. Typical floor plan of a residential block.
4. The Wolfson Building.
5. Corridor and staircase on the top floor.
6. View of a study-bedroom.

Arup Associates
Wolfson Building, Somerville College, Oxford, 1966

The Wolfson Building for twenty undergraduates and three fellows completes the enclosure of Somerville's large quadrangle. Rooms face on to Walton Street and on to the quad. The staircases are in free-standing brick towers at each end of the block and form links between the new concrete structure and its older neighbours.
Beams of a depth appropriate to a 33-foot span over the hall at ground level are bolted to pairs of columns. In terms of the study-bedroom the wide bay frames the window, the narrow one screens the bed. The window projecting beyond the line of columns forms a lookout post and provides good light for the working wall that carries desk and bookshelves.

1

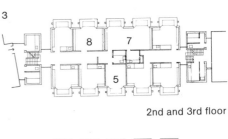

2nd and 3rd floor

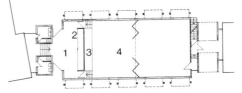

1st floor

Ground floor

2

1. The building as an element in the street.
2. The building as an element in the quadrangle.
3. Plans. Key: 1 lobby, 2 cloaks, 3 stage, 4 hall, 5 bedroom, 6 study/bed, 7 study/living, 8 tutor.
4. Detail of the facade.

Sir Leslie Martin and Colin St John Wilson
Harvey Court, Gonville and Caius College, Cambridge, 1960

This unit of residential accommodation for undergraduates and fellows had to be built on a separate site from the main college, where space for expansion was not available. The building has been conceived to form the nucleus of a later development. The geometry of the square courtyard is deliberately broken, and some of the rooms face outwards, as an anticipation of a larger and looser grouping. The building relies for much of its effect on the resulting tension.

A compact building has been achieved by packing dining room and other service accommodation into the centre, under a podium which forms the courtyard. Construction is of concrete slabs and pieces, which are however concealed in the brickwork.

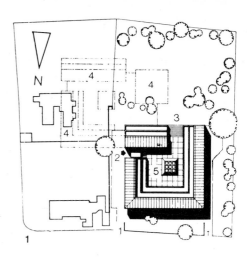

1

2

3

4

5

6

1. Site layout. Key: 1 entrance from the road,
2 main entrance, 3 garden entrance, 4 college
extension, 5 courtyard.
2. The garden entrance.
3. The complex seen from the south.
4. Stepped terraces of individual study-bedrooms.
5. A corner of the courtyard.
6. Access gallery on the ground floor.

Gillespie Kidd & Coia
The Lawns, University of Hull, Cottingham, 1964

The development will eventually consist of twelve halls of residence, a centre with recreational and dining facilities, fourteen houses for staff and a service centre. Six halls, the social and service centres, and three houses for academic staff have been completed. The development has to be relatively self-contained as it is situated in parkland three miles distant from the university, illustrating the difficulty of placing residental units close to teaching units in the congested centres of cities.

The architects have arrived at the subdivision of the accommodation into smaller units by considering its residential character. With the halls they have arrived at a unit comprising accommodation for 135 students and 8 lodgers, 4 tutors, warden and bursar. The group of twelve such halls provides a sufficient pool of demands to justify an extensive social centre.

Visually each hall has been broken down into staggered and raking segments; so that in combination they appear like the clustered houses of an Italian hill village.

The structure is in brickwork, with intermediate floors of concrete and roofs in timber. The recessed balconies afford privacy and protection against airborne noise.

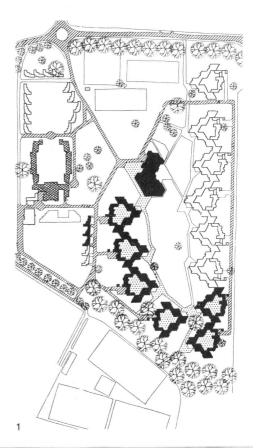

1

2

1. Site layout.
2. Distant view under construction.
3. View from the outermost hall towards the centre.
4. Typical floor plan of a residential unit. Key:
1 study-bedroom, 2 double study-bedroom, 3 parlour, 4 tutor's study-bedroom, 5 tutor's sitting and dining room, 6 senior common room, 7 housekeeper's office, 8 warden's office, 9 sitting room, 10 dining room, 11 kitchen, 12 guest bedroom.

3

4

50'

20m

Powell and Moya
Cripps Building, St John's College, Cambridge, 1964

In much of today's building programme, the architects are asked to meet immediate needs as cheaply as possible with a short-life fabric. In this case the wish of the college was for a building which would match up to the famous buildings of the city, be capable of adaptation by future generations, and last five hundred years. The architects have responded to these requirements in a positive way: the building is of large scale, as many of the central colleges in Cambridge are. Although linear in form, it creates courtyards by setbacks which relate to the positions of the existing buildings surrounding it. Broken masses on the roofline, together with setbacks on plan, create a varied silhouette and avoid the disturbing effect which might have resulted from introducing a bland mechanical regularity in association with the accidental play of turrets, pinnacles and chimneys in the surrounding buildings.

The structure is a reinforced concrete frame with clear spans which will permit flexibility in future adaptations. The building is clothed almost entirely in Portland stone, although the slab edges are in specially finished concrete. Careful attention to landscape — trees, grass and water — has given the whole a rich and varied character.

1
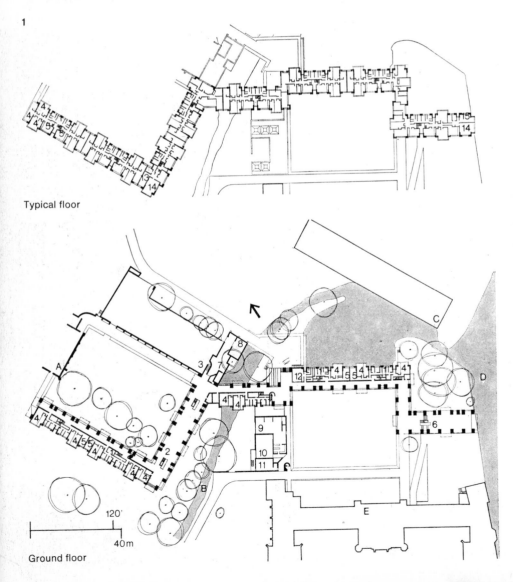

Typical floor

Ground floor

120'

40m

2

1. Plans. Key: 1 gyps and bath, 2 cloisters, 3 parking, 4 undergraduate room (type 1), 5 undergraduate room (type 2), 6 covered open space, 7 refuse, 8 plant, 9 junior common room, 10 terrace, 11 seminar room, 12 porter, 13 fellow's study, 14 fellow's keeping, 15 fellow's bedroom; A School of Pythagoras, B Bin Brook, C Magdalene Building, D River Cam, E New Court.
3. View looking west from School of Pythagoras.
4. View looking south with junior common room in the foreground.

3

4

Attenborough + Jones
Athlone Hall and Cameron Hall, Royal Holloway College, Englefield Green, 1966

This is a group of two similar halls of residence sited in parkland close to the parent building — an 1890 edition of the château of Chambord. Each hall has its own separate dining and common rooms. As the ground slopes quite steeply and there are fine views the halls have been placed in line, one behind and above the other. The space between the two buildings is free from traffic, as the services, administration, kitchens and dining halls are placed at the western end of each range.

The structure of the residential blocks is of load-bearing grey concrete block walls with concrete floor slabs. The larger social spaces have a concrete frame, with a facing of concrete blocks. Finishes are of a modest standard; fixed windows are in simple deal frames but opening lights are in sliding aluminium frames.

1

2

3

4

1. Axononometric view.
2. General view.
3. The rear of the upper hall.
4. Open space between the halls.

1

Howell, Killick, Partridge and Amis
University Centre, Cambridge, 1964

The University Centre is a meeting place for all senior members of the university, whether
dons, masters of colleges, research graduates, administrative staff, wives or husbands.
The programme of accommodation is rather like that of a large London club, with dining
rooms and lounges arranged for relaxation and enjoyment.
In order to preserve some old cottages which occupied part of the site, the architects
have designed a compact rectangular building, in which the largest volume — the principal dining hall — is placed at the back of the site with its kitchens and service rooms,
leaving the frontage with pleasant views of the riverside for common rooms.
The structure consists of a precast concrete frame, post-tensioned and locked together
by the *in situ* concrete floors. The free-standing columns in the common rooms give
domestic scale to large spaces, and conversely the expression of these articulations
on the main river facade gives large scale on the exterior, and a uniform rhythm on
two at least of the faces. Interest in the dining hall is maintained by a strenuous roof
structure and lantern.

2

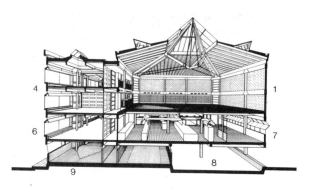

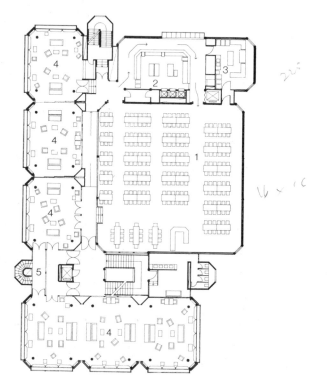

3

4

5

91

1, 2. The building seen from the river.
3. Section and second floor plan. Key: 1 dining hall, 2 kitchen, 3 washing-up area, 4 common room, 5 escape balcony, 6 small dining rooms, 7 kitchen, 8 parking, 9 snack-bar.
4. Common room.
5. The dining hall on the second floor.

1

Ralph Erskine
Clare Hall, Cambridge, 1966

This is a combination of residential, social and work places for scholars of all ages, with or without families. There are three main divisions: a residential block to the rear containing flats of various sizes, a band of small houses with small courts between, and a block comprising bar, common rooms, studies and seminar rooms. The flats build up in height from south to north, with an external access gallery climbing up parallel to the highest doors; including the houses there are in all twenty dwelling units of six different sizes.
Construction is of load-bearing brickwork with filled cavities, and insulated timber roof with aluminium sheet covering. Untreated pine boarding is used for ceilings in most of the communal spaces.

92

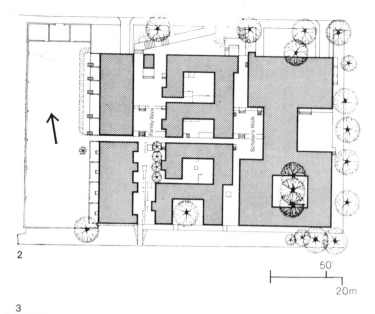

2

3

4

5

1. The residential block seen from the west.
2. Site layout.
3. Southern entrance to the 'Family Walk'.
4. The 'Family Walk'.
5. The houses seen from the high gallery of the residential block.

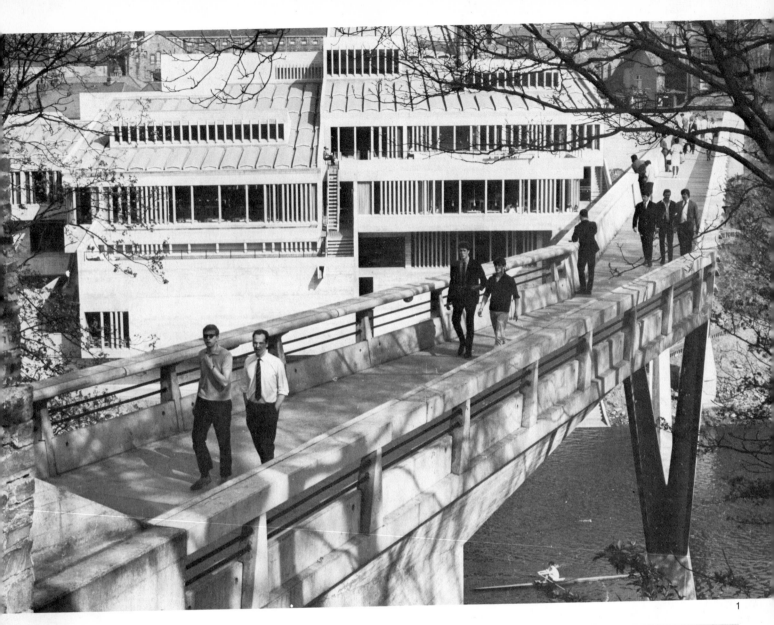

1

2

Architects' Co-Partnership
Dunelm House, Durham University, 1964

This social building houses the student club and the university staff house. It is situated on a dramatic site on the steep banks of the River Wear, half-way between the older university precinct beside the cathedral and the newer development south of the old city. The adjacent footbridge by Ove Arup is part of the pedestrian route joining these two areas.

The building is neatly dug into the sloping bank, its falling roofline dissimulating a considerable volume of accommodation within a modest envelope. All the main spaces are linked by a main staircase which traverses the whole building in a single line, leading from the main entrance at the top to the dance hall at the bottom.

The structure is almost entirely of reinforced concrete. The roof consists of lapping precast concrete units. Internal finishes are simple and robust, with sound absorbants and lighting concentrated in the ceilings.

The dramatic site and the building are greatly enhanced by Ove Arup's footbridge across the Wear. By keeping the level of the bridge high, the design exploits the bracing effect of the slender diagonal struts.

4

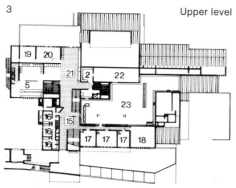

3   Upper level

5

Central level

Lower level

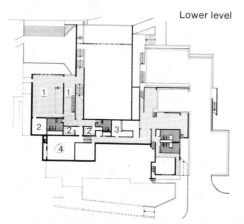

5

1. View from across the River Wear to Dunelm House.
2. The footbridge and the cathedral.
3. Plans. Key: 1 hall, 2 store, 3 beer and wine store, 4 heating room, 5 bar, 6 cloakroom, 7 cafeteria, 8 servery, 9 kitchen, 10 staff dining room, 11 lounge, 12 guest room, 13 table tennis room, 14 billiard room, 15 entry, 16 bedroom, 17 office, 18 conference room, 19 bridge room, 20 reading room, 21 foyer, 22 plant room, 23 roof garden.
4; 5. The building seen from the street.

James Stirling
Andrew Melville Hall, St Andrews University, 1964

The university wants to provide additional accommodation for a regular expansion of student numbers by building four halls of residence consecutively. The present building was therefore designed as a prototype. The ultimate plan envisages two groups of two halls each, each hall having two wings, with communal accommodation at the junction. The halls, each for some 250 students of both sexes, are sited along the edge of a ridge dropping to flat land (originally the sea coast). A main staircase links the entrance at the cliff top to the promenade level, half-way down, from which separate staircases lead up and down to sets of eight study-bedrooms. All the rooms are aligned so that one window has a view of the sea coast to the south.
The service road is at the level of the main promenade, which is conceived as the main socializing space, linking directly to the common rooms.
The precast structured wall elements are cast in a mould lined with ribbed aluminium, the pattern being alternated to provide a clear visual articulation of the separate elements.

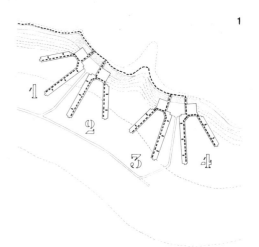

3

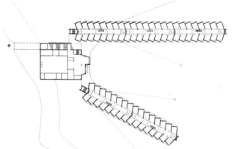

Typical floor

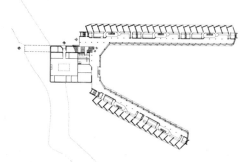

4

Promenade floor

1. Development plan. Only one hall has been completed as yet.
2, 3. General views.
4. Plans.
5. Promenade.

5

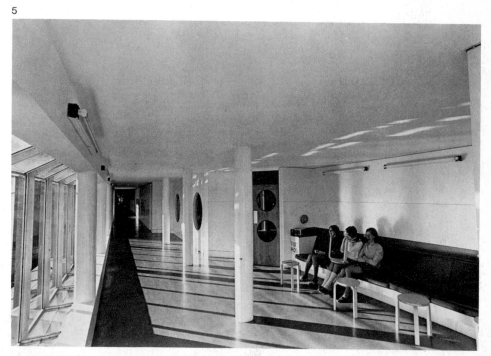

James Stirling
Florey Building, Queens College, Oxford, 1968

This building comprises some seventy-four study-bedrooms for undergraduates, three rooms for research fellows and one apartment for a fellow. The rooms all face on to a courtyard which itself faces north towards the river and towards views of Oxford. The rooms are raised on structural legs and at ground level a cloister runs around under the building, with access to the paved courtyard. A breakfast room, accessible from the west end of the cloister, projects into the corner of the court forming a raised terrace. The main staircase and lifts are drawn away from the building on the south-east face.

The building is constructed in a concrete frame, with red brick facing, and windows in regular patent glazing with opening lights restricted to louvres. Aluminium fabric roller blinds can be individually adjusted for privacy. The corridors on the sunny sides contain all the storage and toilet facilities and also, at intervals, wider spaces for taking tea and fraternizing.

1

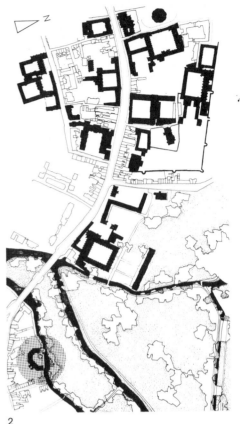

2

1. The courtyard seen from the covered walkway.
2. Site layout.
3. Model.
4. Plans.
5. Section.
6. Detail section through second and third floor.

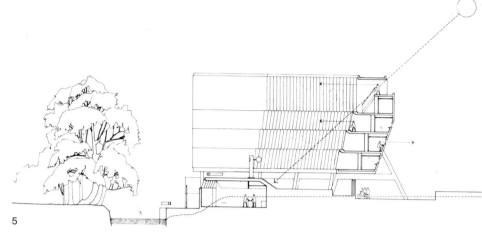

3

4

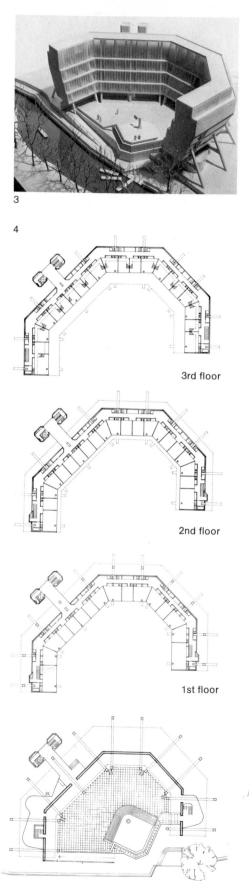

3rd floor

2nd floor

1st floor

Ground floor

5

6

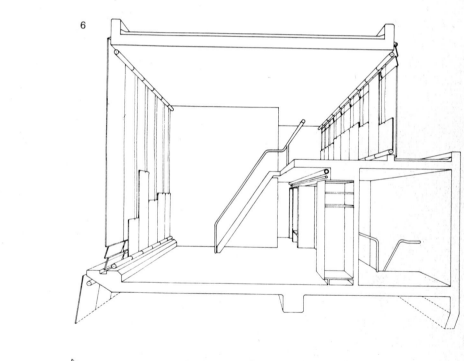

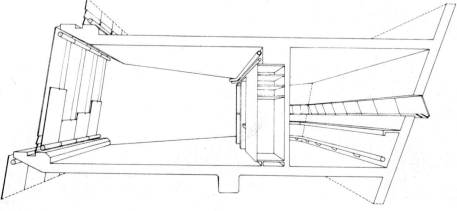

William Whitfield
Library, University of Glasgow, 1965

Only half of the library has been completed, but this represents the essential outline of the building which is seen from the main approaches to the university area. The requirements of the librarian were for a simple 'warehouse' plan, with large floors free from impediment. This gave rise to a rather deep building whose cubic bulk seemed at variance with other elements of the city scape, and particularly with the original library building by Gilbert Scott. The architect has solved the external problem by arranging all his service elements in the form of towers attached to and surrounding the main floor plan. By variation of profile and height, the ring of towers succeeds in camouflaging the regular volume behind. Internally, the plan produces large flexible areas at the expense of rather indirect movement between floors. The corner and central bays of the main reading areas have voids on alternate levels gaining a measure of openness between floors, without directly helping internal circulation. In addition the corner bays are projected, adding elements of the main function to the array of towers on the facade.

1

2

1. General view from the south-east.
2. General view from the south.
3. Bookstack.
4. Reading area.
5. Plans. Basement key: 1 staff cloakroom, 2 bindery preparation, 3 bindery, 4 machine room, 5 microfilm, 6 office, 7 darkroom, 8 finishing, 9 store, 10 plant, 11 janitor, 12 workroom, 13 rare books, 14 newspapers, 15 microfilm cubicles, 16 microfilm, 17 book conveyor, 18 readers' cloakroom, 19 temporary main entrance. Entrance level key: 1 temporary plant, 2 issue desk, 3 reception, 4 deputy librarian, 5 exhibition, 6 office, 7 inter-library loans, 8 Hunterian collection, 9 catalogue, bibliography and reference, 10 plant, 11 staff entrance, 12 loading bay, 13 book acquisitions, 14 official catalogues, 15 sub-librarian, 16 cataloguing and classification, 17 book conveyor. Second floor key: 1 blind readers' room, 2 staff cloakroom, 3 double study room, 4 single study room, 5 seminar room, 6 office, 7 emergency exit, 8 bookstacks and reading areas, 9 void, 10 plant, 17 book conveyor.

5

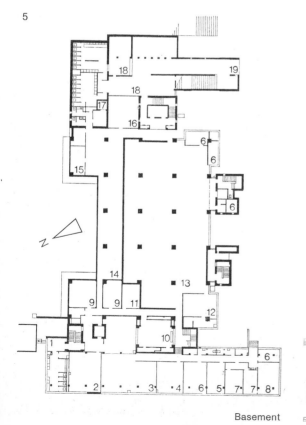

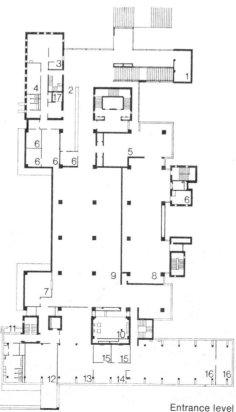

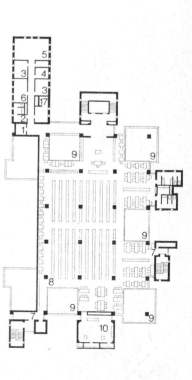

Basement

Entrance level

2nd floor

Sir Leslie Martin, Colin St John Wilson; Patrick Hodgkinson, Douglas Lanham
Library group, Oxford University, 1963

This group of libraries includes the Bodleian Law Library, the English Faculty Library, and the Institute of Statistics Library. In each library a reading room extending through an upper galleried floor to a high top-lit space forms the main element of the plan, and it is surrounded by secondary bookstacks and study rooms. At the lower levels there are lecture theatres and seminar rooms. The three libraries are grouped together about an external public staircase, from the different levels of which the various reading rooms are approached. Although each high volume is square in plan, the different libraries interlock together in a way which does not distinguish the different entities, but rather unifies them in a free and picturesque composition.

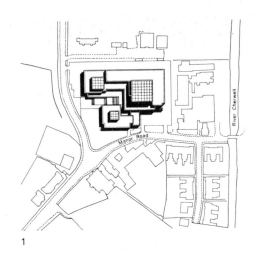

1

2

3

1st floor

3rd floor

Ground floor

2nd floor

4

1. Site layout.
2. The main approach stair.
3. The Bodleian Law Library.
4. Plans. Key: 1 carrels, 2 Law Library gallery, 3 English gallery, 4 wing stack, 5 junior common room, 6 kitchen, 7 senior common room, 8 workspace, 9 microfilm, 10 Law Library stack, 11 secretary, 12 librarian, 13 entrance hall, 14 study, 15 seminar, 16 cataloguing, 17 reading room, 18 WC, 19 staff common room, 20 binding, 21 porter, 22 Statistics gallery, 23 research room, 24 courtyard, 25 director, 26 office, 27 punched card, 28 computing, 29 lecture theatre, 30 lecture room, 31 plant room, 32 receiving and packing, 33 office, 34 Statistics Library reading room, 35 janitor's flat.

Castle Park Dean Hook
Reconstruction and extension of Brynmor Jones Library, University of Hull, 1965

The reconstruction and extension represents an enlargement of the library services by about 200%, and an even larger increase in book capacity.

The new West Building is linked to the remainder only at ground and first floor levels. It is ten floors high. The basement and lower ground floor are given over to mechanical and administrative services. The ground floor contains catalogue, conference and reading rooms, and staff offices. Periodicals are on the first floor, the specialized law library on the second, and the remaining floors, characterized by a continuous cantilevered way with horizontal strip windows, each contain a central bookstack surrounded by reading areas. Stairs, lifts and other services are concentrated on one side of the square volume, which is carried on concrete columns arranged on a square grid of 8.23 m. (27 ft.).

The environment is completely artificially lit and air-conditioned, and the windows are viewing strips rather than conventional windows. They are fixed double-glazed units canted to 60° to reduce solar heat gain. The white cladding above and below the windows is in vitreous enamelled steel, while the concrete structural slab is picked out with brown glazed tiles.

1

2

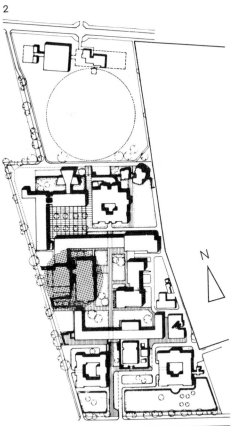

1. The new building seen from the south.
2. Site layout.
3. The new building seen from the east.
4. Plans and section. Key: 1 access, 2 entrance hall, 3 cloakroom, 4 reserve collection, 5 lower reading room, 6 catalogue, 7 bibliography and reference, 8 catalogue workroom, 9 reference reading room, 10 bookstack.

3

4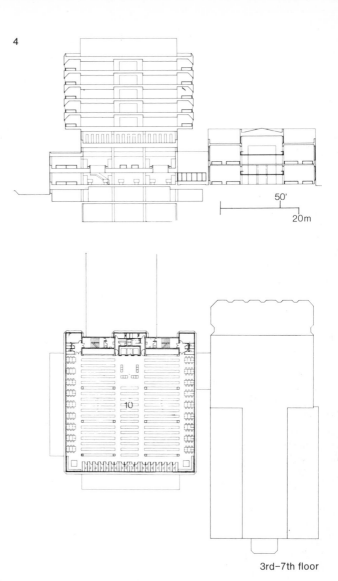

50'

20m

3rd–7th floor

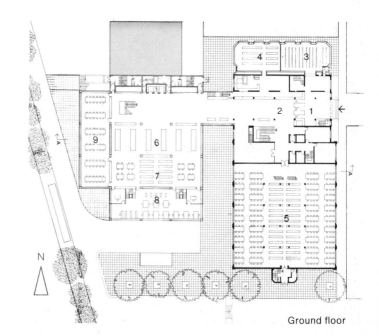

N

Ground floor

5, 6. Reading areas in the upper part of the new building.

1

Renton Howard Wood Associates
Edinburgh College of Domestic Science, Clermiston, 1971

Strictly speaking this is not a university building, but a self-contained college, with its own teaching, administrative and residential accommodation. The grounds are extensive, with ample space for future growth, and with a regular natural slope, good views and specimen trees. The architects have made a development plan using a basic L-shaped formation, in which one arm is always free to expand, and creating spaces open to view and sun to the south and west, while sheltered by the building masses in the north and east.

The northern L comprises in its narrow wing the bulk of the teaching accommodation, arranged on five levels. The main halls, lecture theatres and administration spaces are arranged in the deeper wing. To the south, further L-shaped masses comprise the residential accommodation; two of these are conventional halls of residence, the third one is arranged as blocks of flats.

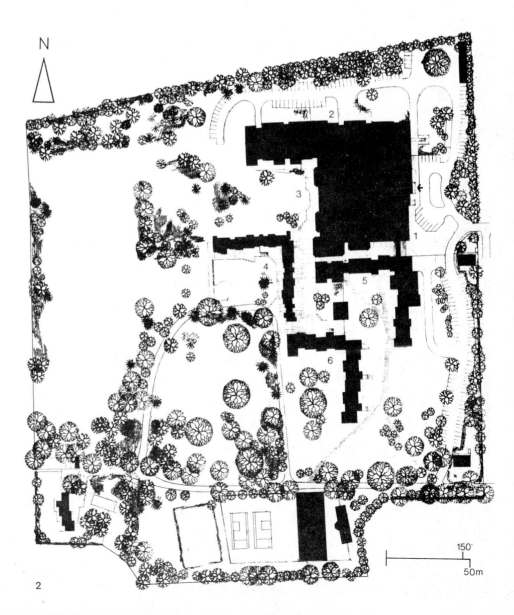

2

1. Model.
2. Site layout. Key: 1 administration, 2 teaching wing, 3 communal area, 4 student flats, 5, 6 student rooms.

3. The teaching wing seen from the north-east.
4. The teaching wing seen from the north-west.
5. The communal area seen from the west.
6. The refectory in the southern part of the communal area.

Arup Associates
Loughborough University of Technology, 1967

In this university the great majority of subjects to be studied have exacting requirements for laboratory space, disposable in large units, flexible and highly serviced. It is this over-riding aspect which has dictated the adoption of a regular planning module, consisting of a unit of space of approximately 15 m. (46 ft.) square, using deep precast girders supported at the corners. These units can be stacked to form storeys and extended horizontally in chequer-board pattern. The major units are separated by a link unit some 3.2 m. (10 ft. 6 in.) wide, without separate structure. This absence of structure in the link allows horizontal addition to be effected without disturbance to the existing units. The deep girders allow the service connection to reach all parts of the plan.

2

1

1. Roof terraces are formed on the projecting wings, taking advantage of view and sun.
2. Detail of facade.
3. The laboratory building seen from the east.
4. Site layout. Key: 1 teaching building, 2 laboratory building, 3 post-graduate building.
5. The deep girders allow the service connection to reach all parts of the plan.

3

4

5

Lyons Israel Ellis Partnership
Polytechnic College of Engineering and Science, London, 1967

This building houses the teaching accommodation for six disciplines — mechanical and electrical engineering, mathematics, physics, chemistry and biology — on an extremely restricted site. The main teaching block is on the east flank, the smaller block facing south contains mainly tutorial and seminar rooms. The lecture halls, communal spaces and dining room are attached to the entrance zone which separates the two blocks, and the basement is occupied by workshops and parking.

In terms of abstract composition, the building is articulated by the lecture theatres, staircase and lift towers, whose blank masses contrast with the regular fenestration of the remainder. The volumes are close-knit and highly integrated, and this expression appears to correspond to a synthesizing rather than an analytical interpretation of the activity patterns and their spatial organization.

The structure is of reinforced concrete throughout. Exposed surfaces are finished in a special white aggregate with regular shutter marks. The floors are in precast units comprising service ducts. The glazing is carried out in light section bronze curtain walling, which harmonizes with bronze-tinted glass and with the cream tiles used to surface the terraces and entrance courts.

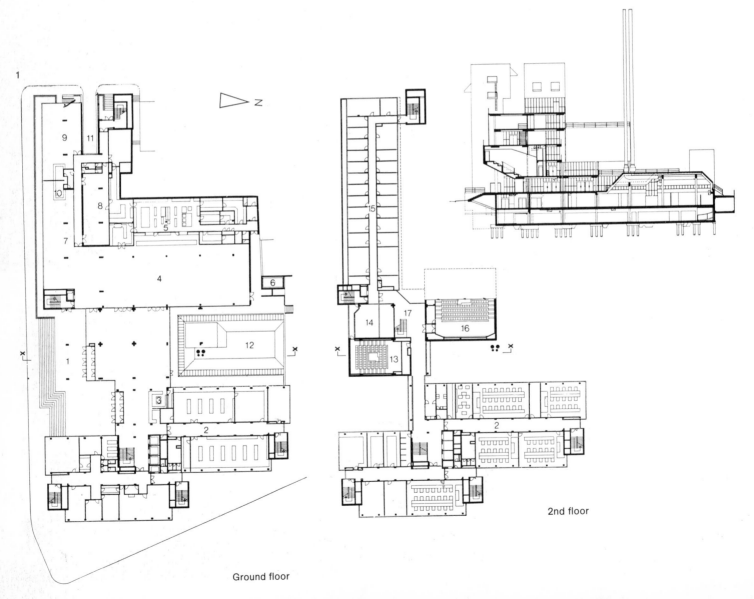

Ground floor

2nd floor

2

3

4

1. Plans and section. Key: 1 main entrance, 2 laboratory block, 3 porter, 4 dining room, 5 kitchen, 6 hoist, 7 students' common room, 8 staff dining room, 9 staff common room, 10 bar, 11 ramp to car park, 12 thermo-dynamics, 13 small lecture theatre, 14 open well, 15 tutorial block, 16 large lecture theatre, 17 stair to library.
2. General view of the complex seen from the north-east.
3. View from the east.
4. View from the south-east.

3

5. The entrance court.
6. The library.
7. The dining room.
8. The entrance concourse.

6

7

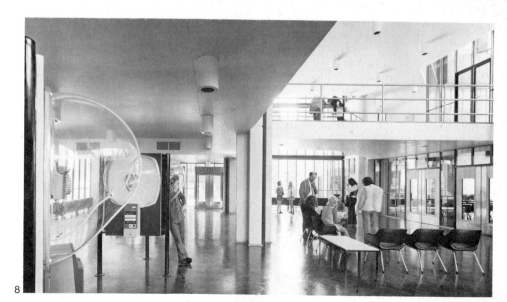

8

James Stirling, James Gowan
Engineering laboratories, Leicester University, 1960

The main requirement was for extensive teaching workshops, some of which required very heavy equipment, and in addition research laboratories, lecture theatres, staff rooms and administration. The workshops cover most of the area of a restricted site, and this was the main reason for piling up all the other accommodation into a cluster of towers. A large water reservoir with sufficient gravity pressure to serve the needs of the hydraulic engineering workshop is incorporated into the top storey. The workshops at ground level are capable of being extended or subdivided, while the functions accommodated in the tower were not expected to change. Rooflights above the workshops are of insulated glass and are set at 45° to preserve correct orientation for the north lights.

The building is remarkable for its functional severity, its formal originality, and its aggressive assimilation of commonplace materials — bright red brick and patent glazing. Keyed red tiles are used to clothe the concrete where brick would not be possible — such as the soffits of the cantilevered lecture theatres. Similar tiles used on terraces and balustrades give the building great homogeneity and ensure maximum clarity of the forms.

1. The circulation space, totally glazed, steps back at higher levels, throwing into relief the laboratory tower (left) and the office tower (right).
2. Plans.
3. General view of the towers.

1

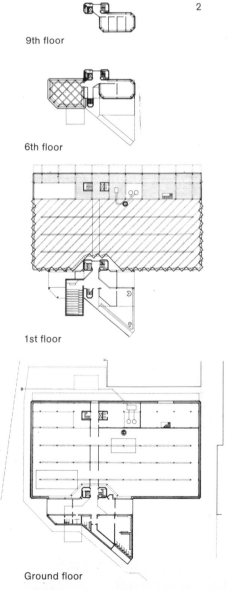

2

9th floor

6th floor

1st floor

Ground floor

11

4

5

6

4. The electronics laboratory (fourth floor of the
low building) showing the rooflights set at 45°.
5. Exterior of the electronics laboratory.
6. A landscape of glass.

1

1

James Stirling in partnership with Michael Wilford
History Faculty Building, Cambridge, 1964

The main requirement for this building was a large reading room for 300 readers, along with staff rooms, seminar rooms and common rooms. The reading room with its catalogue and control spaces occupies most of the ground floor. Above it, on two sides, rise six storeys of smaller rooms, forming an L-shaped block, into the angle of which rises the glazed roof of the reading room. Twin towers containing staircase and lifts rise against the north face, adjacent to the main entrance point.
The glazed roof of the reading room is carried on four raking tubular steel welded lattice girders. The inner glass is largely insulated and the space between skins is capable of natural ventilation. Three large fans extract used warm air from the apex of the space to the outside.
Internal windows to the corridors of the teaching block allow users in each half of the building to be aware of the other. With so much visual interest in the structure, internal finishes have been kept very simple — white plaster and natural wood. The external surfaces are finished in red brick or patent glazing.

2

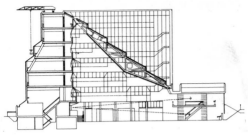

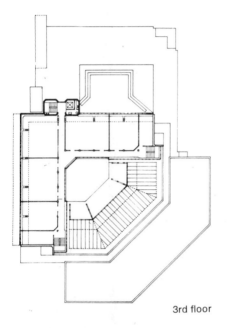

3rd floor

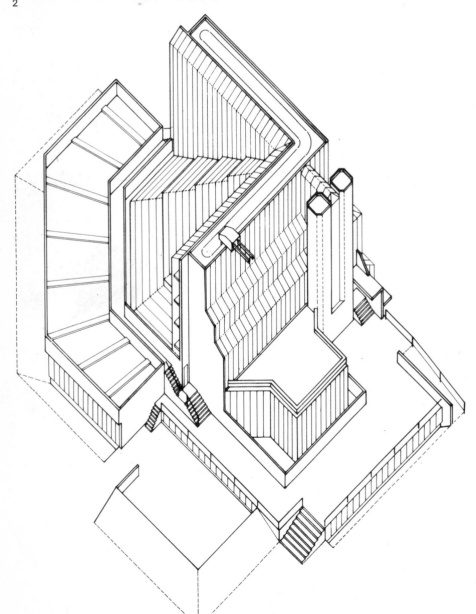

3

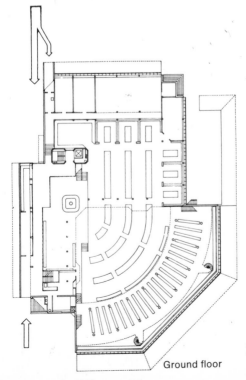

Ground floor

4   12

2. View from the west.
3. Axonometric view.
4. Plans and section.
5. View down from the top level.
6, 7. Views up towards the apex of the reading room.

5

7

6

Sir Basil Spence, Bonnington & Collins
Falmer House and Physics Building, University of Sussex, 1960

These two buildings were the first to be completed in the development of the new campus of the University of Sussex.

Falmer House is the social focus of the university, and contains refectories, common rooms and recreation rooms. The regular form of the courtyard is broken by the projecting volumes of the refectory and the debating hall, and it is penetrated by many openings in the ground floor. The structure is of load-bearing brick cross walls, with concrete slabs and vaults. The outside space is glimpsed from the courtyard between the rather massive brickwork supports rather than flowing freely.

The Physics Building has a similar vocabulary of vaulted spaces, but the structure is simple, as it follows a single direction on all four sides. As the site is sloping, the section varies in height from three storeys to one under a uniform roofline. At the single-storey side, a wing is intended to be added later on the opposite side of the street.

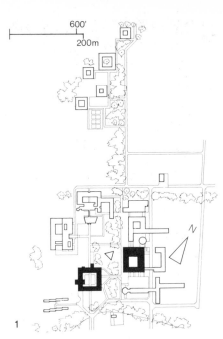

1

2

3

4

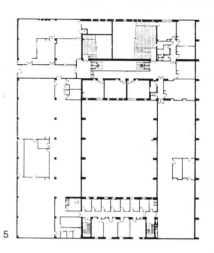

5

6

7

1. Site layout.
2. Falmer House seen from the east.
3. The inner courtyard of Falmer House.
4. Plan of Falmer House (first floor).
5. Plan of Physics Building (upper ground floor).
6. Physics Building seen from the south.
7. The inner courtyard of the Physics Building.

Richard Sheppard, Robson & Partners
Central Lecture Theatre, Brunel University, 1966

This block of lecture theatres serves the needs of the whole Brunel campus, grouped in one place to maximize efficiency of use. There are a large range of rooms of various sizes, three theatres seating 180, three seating 100, sixteen seating 60 and classrooms seating 10–40. The theatres are mechanically ventilated and artificially lit to reduce disturbance from aircraft noise.

The six larger theatres are grouped at the northern end, where they dominate the main pedestrian square. The remaining theatres are placed in the centre of the building mass, surrounded by the classrooms, which have natural light and ventilation. There are large concourses at ground floor, first floor and gallery level. All levels have a small servery for light refreshments between lectures. On the ground floor at the south end are two large reading and writing rooms.

The structure is a combination of concrete and brick. Precast concrete cladding panels are cast with a Cornish granite aggregate.

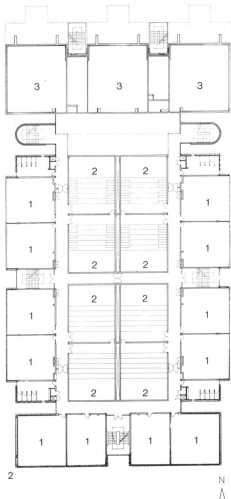

1

2

1. The view along the north face, under the over-hangs of the lecture theatres.
2. Plan of the second floor. Key: 1 classroom, 2 lecture theatre, 3 void.
3. The complex viewed from the south-east.
4. The main concourse, with lecture theatres on the right, and upper concourse galleries above.
5. A corner of the reading room on the south side.

1

3

4

5

5

Robert Matthew, Johnson-Marshall and Partners
Bath University of Technology, 1966

The university is sited some two miles from Bath, on a hillside with slopes to the south. As the situation is isolated, the design has been conceived for compactness, while allowing for growth. This is made possible by adopting a linear spine, to which the various departments connect, the outer ends open for future expansion. The slope allows the spine to function at two levels — a service road below, and a pedestrian deck above, which is sometimes spanned by building blocks. Next to the deck the architects situated the communal areas, the general departments and the main part of student residences, while more specialized teaching buildings are placed on the outside with the heavy laboratory farthest away.

Construction varies, but is generally of concrete frame with prefabricated cladding. Later sections have been carried out in the JDP system sponsored by the University Grants Committee together with the Department of Education and Science.

2

1. The Electrical Engineering School, constructed in the JDP building system, is less genial in appearance than the earlier parts.
2. General view from the south.
3. Site layout.
4. A building spanning the pedestrian deck.

3

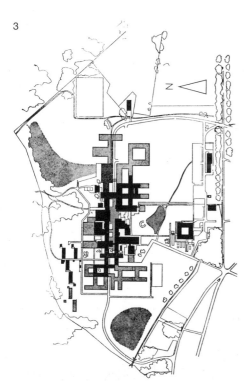

4

Denys Lasdun & Partners
University of East Anglia, 1964

This is another university complex situated in rural isolation — about a mile west of Norwich, on a splendid site with slopes to the south and many mature trees. The architect has conceived the built form as a kind of urban landscape, combining the man-made qualities of building with the natural qualities of hills and views. The organization is by means of a pedestrian spine, with a walkway at constant level independent of the ground; this will be flanked to the north-west by the main teaching departments, successively Arts, Chemistry, Mathematics and Physics (not yet constructed), and Biology. South of this is the students' residential accommodation, arranged in a long string of stepped L-shaped blocks. To the east is the general accommodation — computer centre, lecture theatres, library (part built) and administrative centre (not yet built), with a terrace of staff housing closing the complex to the south-east.
The vertical access towers of the residential units rise dramatically behind the terraces when seen from the south, but are not overpowering when seen from the teaching building on account of the advantage these gain from the slope. This varied quality of perception indicates how completely the architect has integrated the land form and the building form into a single landscape, in which the access spine is the most enclosed space.
The predominant structural means is precast concrete.

1

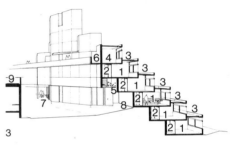
3

2

1. Western termination of the western residential block with Biology Building behind.
2. The comparatively modest scale of the residential units is seen in this view from the north.
3. Section through a residential unit. Key: 1 study-bedroom, 2 corridor, 3 terrace, 4 tutor's flat, 5 services duct, 6 access walkway, 7 entry at road level, 8 cars and bicycles, 9 walkway deck to teaching building.
4. Panoramic view of the first stage completed.
5. Site layout. Key: 1 bus terminus, 2 car park, 3 boiler house, telephone exchange and workshops, 4 Arts, 5 Chemistry, 6 Mathematics and Physics, 7 Biology, 8 Biology garden, 9 students' residences, 10 staff houses, 11 squash courts, 12 library, 13 lecture theatres, 14 university house, 15 computer centre.

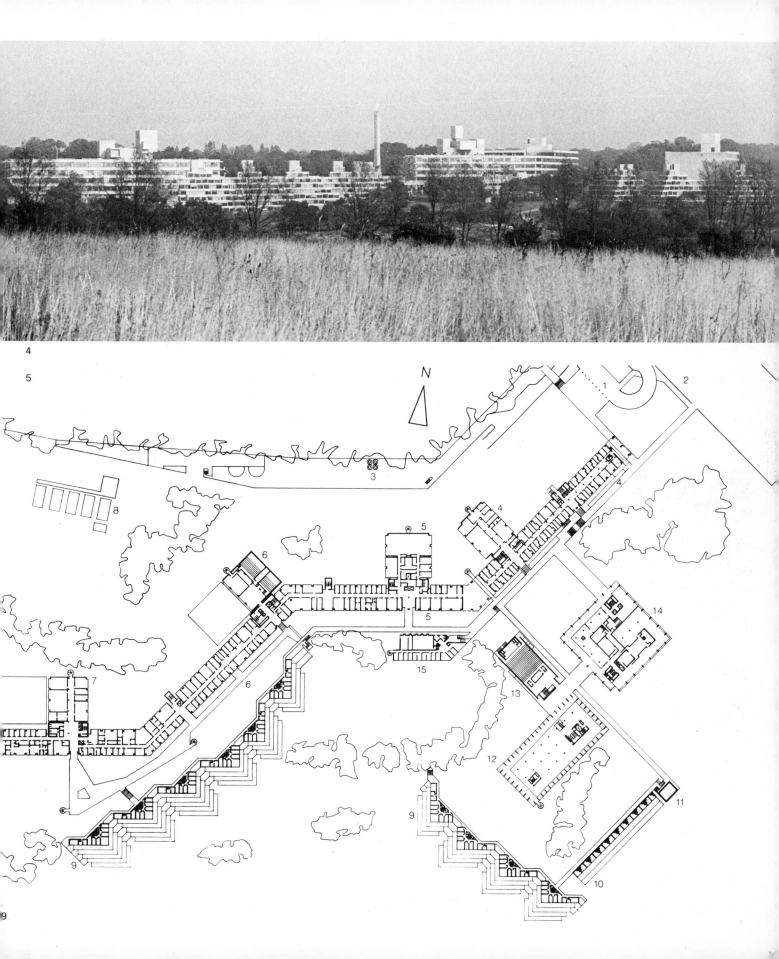

4

5

N

1

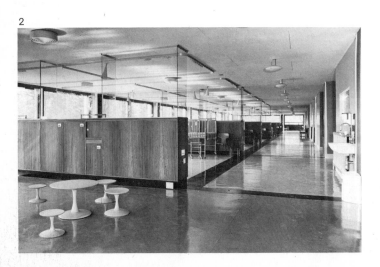

2

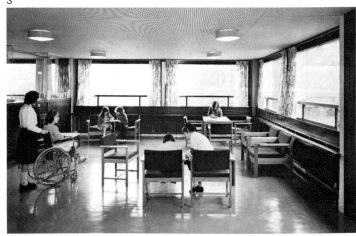

3

Michael Laird and Partners
Children's Clinic, Astley Ainslie Hospital, Edinburgh, 1963

This is a convalescent pavilion for children, situated in south-sloping wooded parkland in the Grange district of Edinburgh. The main block consists of a twenty-bed ward unit on two floors, with play spaces, both covered and enclosed, on the ground floor. There is an observation and physiotherapy wing to the north and a large sun room at roof level.

The wards are organized in four-bed units capable of subdivision into single or two-bed bays. Each ward includes three day rooms, one of which is equipped to double as library and as dining room. A glazed screen over each bed head unit allows easy nursing supervision, while providing a measure of privacy and personal storage for each patient. This storage unit also provides a means of access to the services, which traverse the building on the centre lines of the main structure. The precast concrete beams are paired, joining on to precast H-section concrete columns, to allow the services to share the same gridlines as the structure.

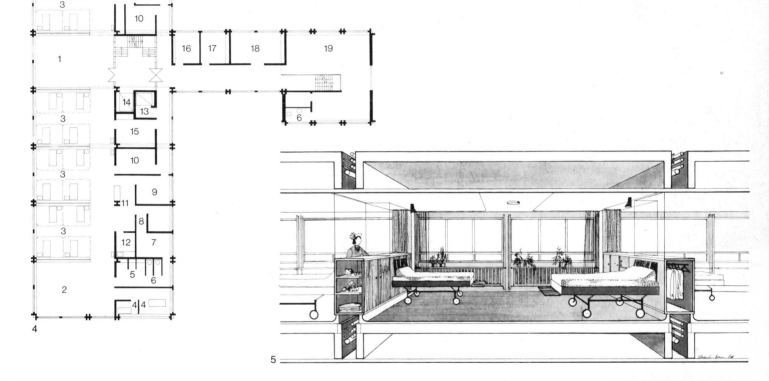

5

6

1. View from the east, with entrance underneath the projecting physiotherapy wing. Note how the twin precast columns are treated at the external corners.
2. General view of a ward unit, with nursing facilities on the right and bed spaces on the left.
3. Day room.
4. Plan of the first floor. Key: 1 dining, day room and library, 2 day room, 3 ward, 4 bathroom, 5 wash-basins, 6 WC, 7 sluice and test, 8 appliance room, 9 clean utility, 10 dirty utility, 11 nurse's station, 12 nurse's room, 13 goods hoist, 14 bed lift, 15 kitchen, 16 sister, 17 doctor, 18 treatment room, 19 physiotherapy.
5. Section through a ward.
6. The building seen from the south.

Llewelyn-Davies Weeks Forestier-Walker & Bor
Northwick Park Hospital and Clinical Research Centre, 1966

The brief for this hospital was unique in combining a major clinical research centre with the requirements of a district general hospital, with the benefits of bringing research workers into better contact with everyday medical problems. At the same time, the development of new clinical methods renders especially important the ability to adapt the building programme to changes in medical practice as well as the normal growth of medical services. The development method, illustrated in the diagrams, is based on a two-level spine linking all the facilities, the upper level being reserved for patients, staff and visitors, the lower level for services and supplies. As the link system traverses or passes free of the building, the buildings are correspondingly free to expand, or alter independently.

Planning, structure and services within the buildings are all based on a modular dimension of 0.864 m. (34 in.) enabling internal walls, pipes and ventilation services to be re-arranged freely. The outside walls are carried on a series of precast concrete mullions which can be spaced economically in relation to the floor loadings. This method provides a rationale for a regular elevational treatment which can nevertheless both vary according to needs and provide architectural unity.

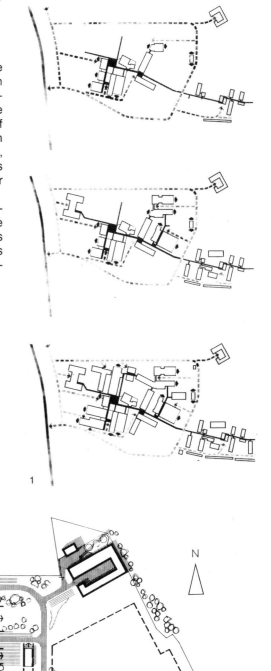

1

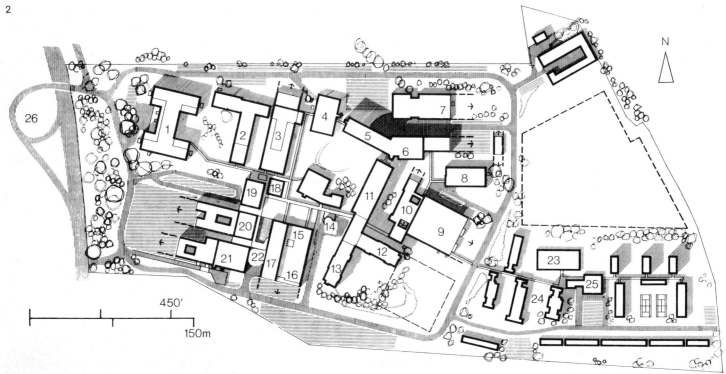

2

3

1. Development schemes.
2. Site layout. Key: 1 maternity unit, 2 psychological medicine, 3 rehabilitation unit, 4 library and lecture hall, 5 medical illustration, 6 clinical research institute, 7 animal house, 8 isolation station, 9 operating theatres, 10 recovery unit, 11, 12, 13 ward building, 14 chapel, 15 pharmacy, 16 x-ray, 17 pathology, 18 shopping square, 19 administration, 20 outpatients' department, 21 accident and emergencies, 22 supplies delivery, 23 school of nursing, 24 staff residences, 25 common rooms, 26 flyover.
3. The ramp by which ambulances reach the accident unit.
4. The ward building on the right, medical illustration building in the background.
5. The operating theatres on the right, ward building in the background.

4

5

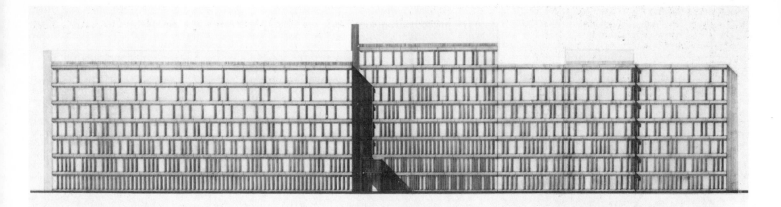

6. The ward building seen from the west.
7. The north end of the ward building. On the left is the clinical research institute.

1

Peter Womersley
Nuffield Transplantation Surgery Unit, Western General Hospital, Edinburgh, 1964

This building houses a unit dealing with organ transplantation in an especially controlled bacteria-free environment. There are three sections: the transplant unit consisting of theatres, ancillaries and recovery rooms for six patients and staff; offices; and an entrance bridge connecting to the radiotherapy unit of the existing hospital. All the zones within the surgery unit are graded in terms of sterility, with an 'aseptic' corridor in the centre and 'dirty' corridors at the periphery, around three sides, the fourth being intended for future expansion of the system.

As the creation of a sterile environment is unusual, the architect has deliberately tried to dramatize this fact by stressing the technical requirements and reflecting them in the formal design. Thus the use of TV monitors to replace direct contact is emphasized by building the sets into regular niches in the external wall. The vaulted beams projecting below the cantilevers are positioned opposite the main air-conditioning ducts and are intended by their shape to express the idea of ducting. The concrete frames are poured *in situ* against fibreglass lined shuttering. The roof is constructed of deep steel trusses. The bridge is also constructed on a deep steel truss, hidden below the precast cladding panels.

2

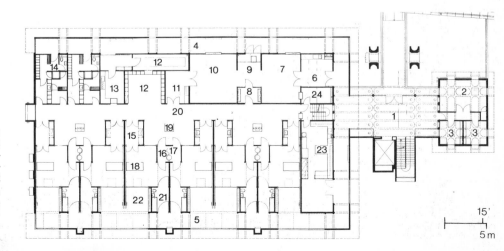

1. General view from the south-east.
2. Plan of the main floor and section. Key: 1 entrance hall, 2 conference room, 3 office, 4 private corridor, 5 visitors' corridor, 6 decontamination, 7 donor theatre, 8 scrub-up, 9 sterilization, 10 recipient theatre, 11 anaesthetic, 12 store, 13 kitchen, 14 changing, 15 entry airlock, 16 exit airlock, 17 disposal chutes, 18 patient, 19 physiological monitor, 20 aseptic corridor, 21 bathroom, 22 observation area, 23 laboratory, 24 disposal.

15'

5 m

3

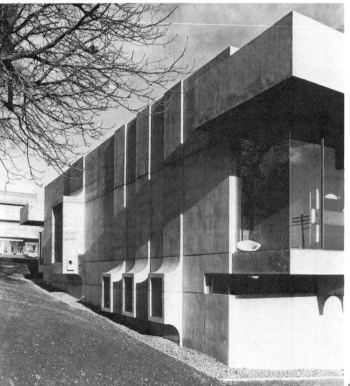

4

3. The new approach road, with the main entrance and bridge connecting to the existing hospital building.
4. Detail of west face. The three openings in the foreground are intakes for the refrigeration plant.
5. The entrance zone.
6. The entrance hall.
7. South face of the patient unit. The large glazed areas light the patients' rooms across the circulation route. Projecting blocks in the first floor house television units.

1

5

6

7

Stillman and Eastwick-Field
Secondary school, Hampstead, London, 1962

This is a new building expanding an existing school. The old buildings have been adapt-
ed and modernized for special uses, enabling the bulk of the general teaching accommodation to be located in the new building. This takes the form of a closed two-storey
courtyard, with teaching spaces in opposite sides, four house rooms served by a single
kitchen at one end, and assembly hall and administrative offices at the other. The falling
ground on the west side has enabled an open undercroft to be placed in such a way
as to link the internal stepped courtyard with the main paved forecourt.
The new addition does not attempt to match with the old red brick building, but is
designed as a simple block, using a regular pattern of precast concrete wall panels
to unify the structure, which is partly of brick cross wall and partly concrete frame.
The cill level of the horizontally glazed metal windows varies in height according to
room uses.

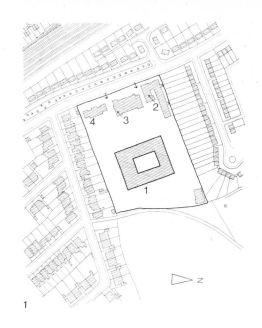

1

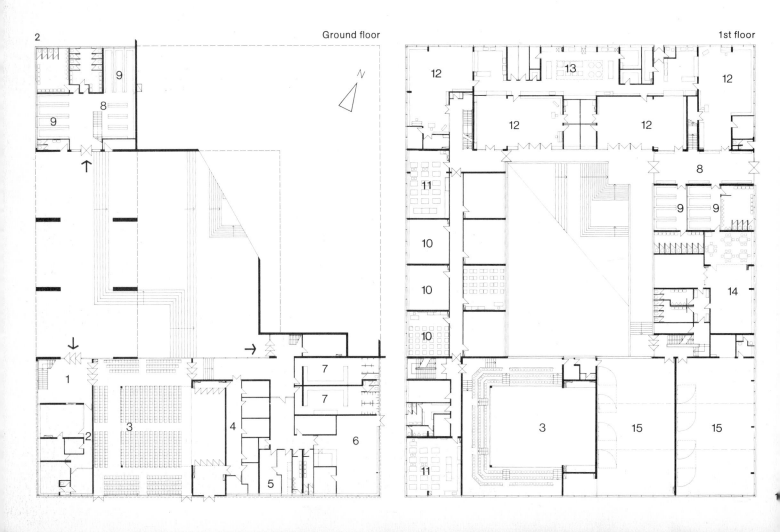

2   Ground floor   1st floor

3

4

5

1. Site layout. Key: 1 new building, 2 swimming pool and gymnasium, 3 main block, 4 science block.
2. Plans. Key: 1 entrance hall, 2 offices, 3 assembly hall, 4 stores, 5 doctor, 6 general purpose room, 7 changing, 8 book lockers, 9 cloakroom, 10 classroom, 11 history, 12 house room, 13 kitchen, 14 teaching staff room, 15 gymnasium.
3. General view.
4. The entrance approach, under the building, to the internal courtyard.
5. The courtyard.

Greater London Council, Department of Architecture and Civic Design
Vittoria Primary School, Islington, London, 1966

This school has been designed as an experiment both in educational policy and in spatial organization. It hopes to extend the catchment area for school starters by providing part-time as well as full-time education in the admission class: it hopes to provide a physical and psychological environment that will stimulate and encourage learning; and specifically to bridge the difficulties of transferring between each level of education (nursery, infant and junior) by associating pairs of classes in adjoining spaces.
The environment has been deliberately broken down into small units. Each classroom unit consists of three spaces, linked by narrow stairs, providing immediate points of reference to the home environment. Since the lowest space includes the eating facilities, each class is treated like a small family. The external organization is also reminiscent of a group of houses, with play courts like private gardens. The construction is of conventional brick cross walls, with light steel framing and dry cladding both internally and externally.

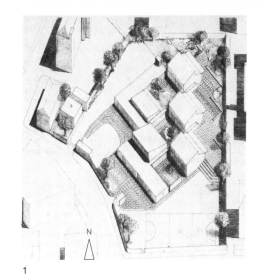

1

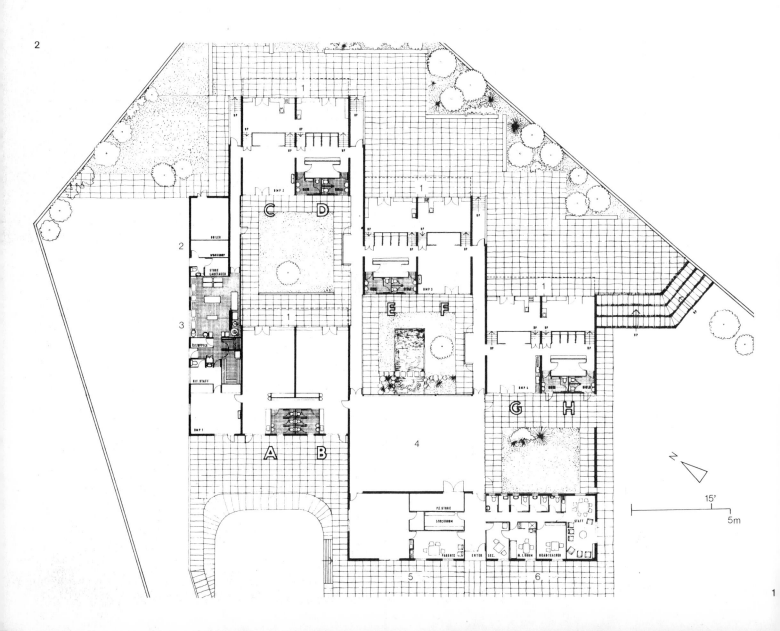

1

3

4

1. Axonometric view.
2. Plan of the ground floor. Key: 1 classroom units,
2 services, 3 kitchen, 4 multipurpose hall, 5 play-
centre, 6 administration.
3. General view from the south-east.
4. The balcony of a classroom. A half level lower
is the 'wet' zone; the lowest level contains a 'noisy'
space, also used for dining.

1

Greater London Council, Department of Architecture and Civic Design
Pimlico Secondary School, London, 1967

This school is situated in a space equivalent to a London square, created by the demolition of two terraces of houses. It is an example of a school planned for maximum compactness and ease of movement. Almost all the accommodation is aligned on the central axis of the site and opens off an internal concourse at first floor level. This is made possible by the ground level being constructed in the volume occupied by the basements of the demolished houses, some 3 m. (9 ft. 10 in.) below the pavement level. The concourse is more a street than a simple corridor, and will be used for exhibition displays and casual meetings. Laboratories, craft rooms, a swimming pool and two gymnasia are arranged on the ground floor, and classrooms on the second and third floor, above the concourse, together with assembly hall, library and common room for senior students.
The structure and external walling are of reinforced concrete with a light-weight aggregate. Columns and cross walls are on a 6.8 m. (22 ft. 4 in.) grid. The concrete is cast from ribbed shuttering. Extensive use has been made of green-house glazing in projecting bays and along the classroom roofs.

1

1. General view from the south-west.
2. View down the long side.
3. Axonometric view.
4. Sections. Key: 3 concourse, 6 classroom, 7 kitchen, 8 assembly hall.
5. Plan of the first floor. Key: 1 entrance, 2 staff and visitors' entrance, 3 concourse, 4 void of gymnasium, 5 void of swimming pool, 6 classroom.
6. Common room.
7. One of the concourses.

2

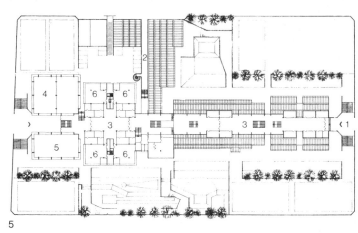

5

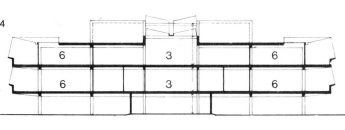

3

6

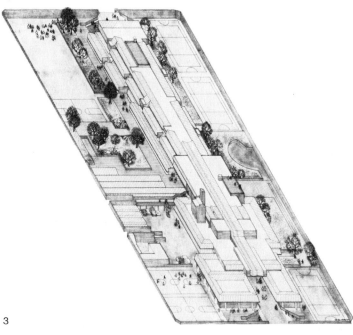

4

7

Howell, Killick, Partridge and Amis
Acland Burghley School, London, 1962

The planning of this school was a difficult problem as the old school buildings occupying the site had to be maintained in use during the building operations. The problem was solved, partly by throwing a concrete deck over the railway cutting which occupied the rear of the site, providing more space, and partly by designing the school as a set of differentiated blocks. This deliberate fragmentation was thought in any case to be a useful feature, as the children might be able to identify with the various parts. In spite of this, all movement about the school can be under cover, and the circulation pattern is the core of the design.

The general classrooms have been grouped into three towers, each identified as the educational base for the lower, middle and upper school. Each contains, at ground level, a pair of dining rooms with service tucked underneath. The more specialist subjects are housed in the longer limb, built over a covered play space, which connects with the games areas to the rear. The administrative block projects at the left of the main entrance, while the assembly hall is situated in the forecourt, where it can be readily used independently of the school.

Structurally the character of the school is defined by the shape of the main facades: a concrete frame on octagonal columns, with flint-faced cladding panels, in part projected above the window strips, resulting in a typically plastic depth of facade.

Ground floor

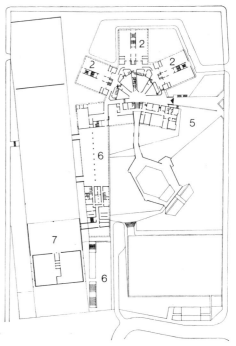

30'

10m

Lower ground floor

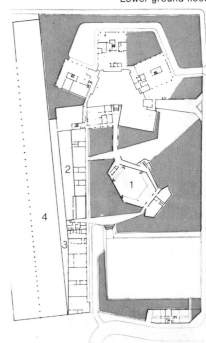

1

2

14

1. Detail of facade.
2. Plans. Key: 1 assembly hall, 2 classrooms, 3 workshops, 4 railway, 5 administration, 6 play, 7 games.
3. Administration and classroom unit. In the foreground a little amphitheatre, on the left the assembly hall.
4. The assembly hall.

3

4

Attenborough + Jones
Swimming pool in Worthing, 1965

This pool forms part of a recreational area on the sea front of Worthing which is managed by the Town Corporation. The main element of the brief is a 33 × 15 m. (108 × 49 ft.) pool, but there is a separate pool for learners and spectator gallery for 500 with a café. Aiming at a compact plan, the architects have positioned the main entrance level with the top tier of spectators' seats, which provides a simple route to their seats and to the cafeteria, leaving the swimmers to make the effort (small compared to their commitment) to descend to their separate changing rooms and clothing store. The way up outside the building is by a ramp and external terrace promenade which conveniently overlooks the existing outdoor pool and recreation zone.
The roof structure is carried on a simple large concrete box frame spanning the main pool hall. From either side of this frame precast concrete through units span longitudinally to concrete posts at either end. Warm air for the pool is distributed through these units. The shape of the roof helps to break up the pool noise, in addition to the acoustic absorbents lining the flat surfaces.

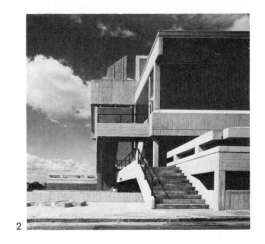

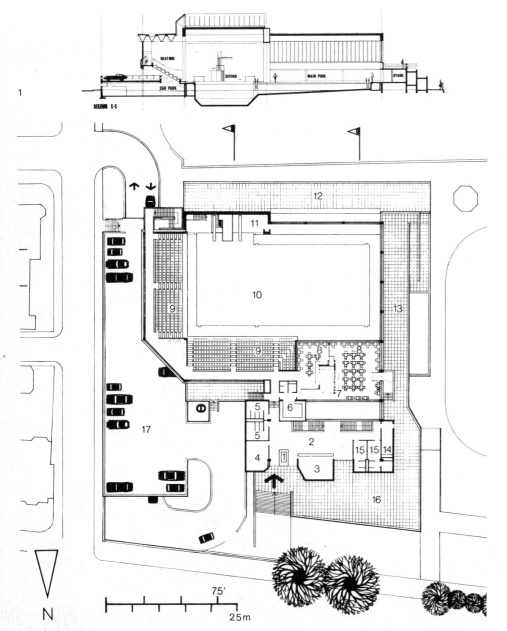

1. Plan of the first floor and section. Key: 1 pay desk, 2 foyer, 3 cloaks, 4 office, 5 WC, 6 kitchen, 7 servery, 8 cafeteria, 9 seating terrace, 10 main pool, 11 diving bay, 12 sunbathing terrace, 13 refreshment terrace, 14 staff room, 15 staff locker room, 16 terrace, 17 upper car park.
2. The building seen from the south-east.
3. The south face.
4. The west face.
5. General view of the pool, looking west.

14

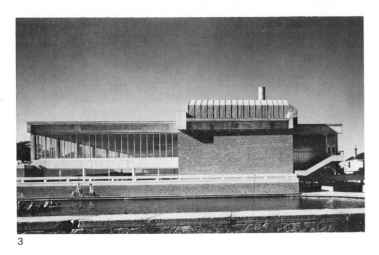

3

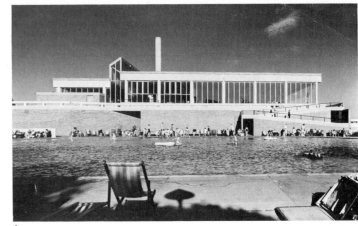

4

5

Peter Womersley
Fairydean Football Club stand, Galashiels, 1963

This stand is designed for a local football club, on an open site surrounded by country-side. The seating (for 620 people) is arranged in a single straight bank, capable of being extended at either end if required. The structure consists of four tapering triangular concrete pylons which support the roof and the back wall of the seating accommodation. The roof cantilevers some 4.5 m. (14 ft. 9 in.) laterally and 7.5 m. (24 ft. 7 in.) forward over the seating. Four strong floodlights are housed within each of the cantilever arms. The back wall of the stand is another triangular box beam, and it also cantilevers 4.5 m. (14 ft. 9 in.) at each end. The front edge of the seating stand is supported from an upstand beam which forms the solid balustrade of the access gallery, at the front of the stand, and this is approached by the two cantilevered staircases, one at either end.

The concrete is cast *in situ* with the board marks left exposed. Continuous glazing to the club rooms on the ground floor accentuates the concentrated role of the main structural supports.

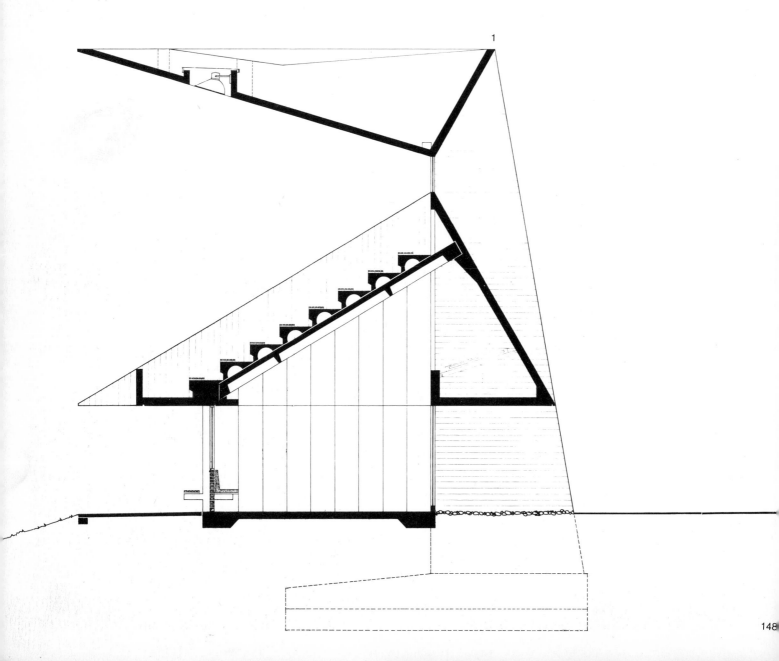

1. Section.
2. The stand seen from the field.
3, 4. Side and rear views.

3

4

Robert Matthew, Johnson-Marshall and Partners
Sailing Club, Grafham Water, Huntingdonshire, 1965

This building provides clubhouse facilities for small boat sailing on Diddington Reservoir, a stretch of water some 5 $\frac{1}{2}$ kilometres (3$\frac{1}{2}$ miles) long by 2$\frac{1}{2}$ kilometres (1$\frac{1}{2}$ miles) wide. The building consists of three floors, each one composed of four by three square bays on a concrete frame, supported at lower levels by brick cross walls. On the ground floor are found the administrative offices, with kitchen and stores. The first floor contains changing rooms and the second floor the clubroom, servery and bars. The roof deck is used as a viewing terrace very much like the bridge of a ship. The external cladding of the concrete frame is of composite reinforced concrete panels, each providing external and internal faces, with the necessary insulation. Windows are mainly in painted frames, with some in aluminium. Heating is by electrical ceiling panels.

2nd floor

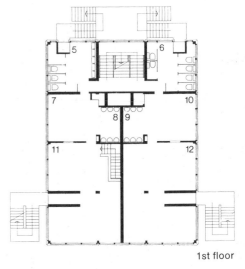

1st floor

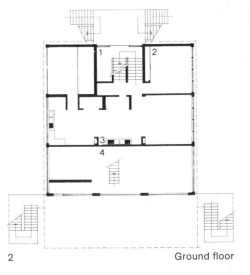

2

Ground floor

1

3

4

1. The main entrance is by external stairs to a half level landing, with further flights giving external access to the changing rooms.
2. Plans. Key: 1 entrance, 2 secretary, 3 kitchen, 4 men's changing, 5 men's WC, 6 women's WC 7 showers, 8 men's washroom, 9 women's washroom, 10 shower, 11 men's changing, 12 women's changing, 13 servery, 14 bar, 15 dining room.
3. The large windows of the clubroom are in aluminium. The recessed ground floor is used for casual parties.
4. Seen from a distance, the functional appendages – stairs, check-point, etc. – give the building some of the urgency of a ship.

51

H. T. Cadbury-Brown and Partners, in association with Brian Richards
Civic Centre, Gravesend, 1964

The brief for a civic centre combines four main functions: administrative offices, social services, council chamber, and a multi-purpose town hall. In this building these functions while operating most of the time in separation, have been arranged and combined into an architectural and social unity. The two heaviest elements — the hall and the administrative offices — have been placed towards the back of the site, at either side, while the mayoral suite, committee rooms and council chamber have been placed at first floor level, above the main entrance hall, so taking formal precedence.

A most interesting aspect of this design is the means by which the hall has been rendered genuinely flexible and capable of many different uses. It has all the facilities of a stage tower and proscenium, while being flat-floored throughout. The problem is solved by a simple mechanism for tilting the central part of the floor to an angle of 10°, automatically creating an apron stage. The tilting floor is supported on four corner columns, two of which are telescopic. The weight of the floor is counterbalanced by a concrete beam, allowing the change to be effected by a man turning a winch. The space beneath the hall floor is usable as a youth club in both positions.

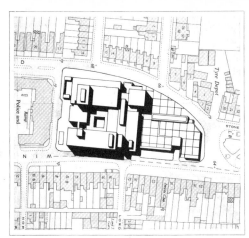

1

2

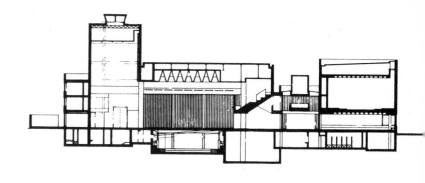

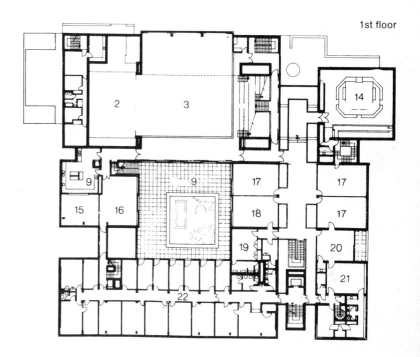

1st floor

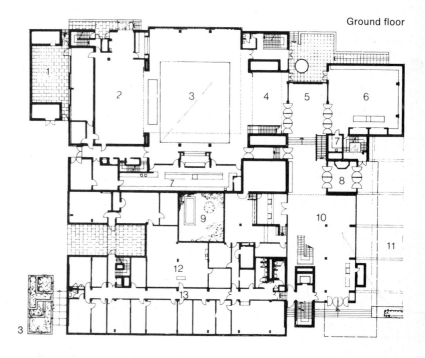

Ground floor

1. Site layout.
2. The main entrance at night.
3. Plans and section. Key: 1 courtyard, 2 stage,
3 assembly hall, 4 back stalls, 5 entrance foyer,
6 reception room, 7 kitchen, 8 entrance lobby,
9 courtyard, 10 entrance foyer, 11 plaza, 12
machine room, 13 offices, 14 council chamber,
15 staff canteen, 16 staff lounge, 17 committee
room, 18 members' room, 19 robing room, 20
reception room, 21 mayor's parlour, 22 offices.

4. The assembly hall arranged as a theatre.
5. Alternative seating arrangements in the hall.
6. The telescopic columns by which the floor is tilted.

4

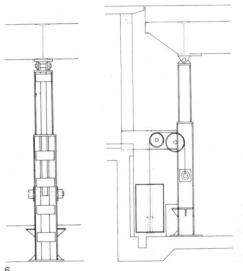

6

5

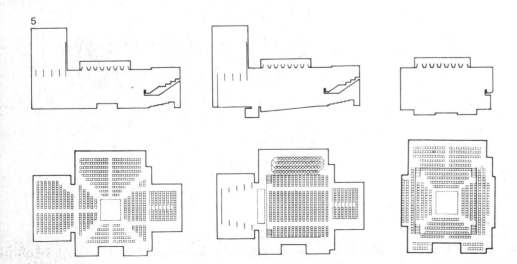

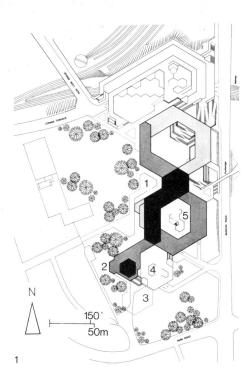

Sir Basil Spence, Bonnington & Collins
Civic Centre, Sunderland, 1968

The site lies on rising ground to the south of the town centre, which it overlooks, although it is isolated from it by an extensive railway cutting. The new centre consists of three principal elements, the largest of which is the administrative offices, for a thousand employees; second in size is the car park; and third in size, if most important socially, is the civic suite, with council chamber, reception rooms, etc.

The whole building has been organized on a triangular grid of approximately 1.5 m. (4 ft. 11 in.), providing a geometry which adapts to the irregular site boundaries. The car park has been placed at the north end where it forms a screen to the railway cutting, while at the same time it creates by its roof terraces a pedestrian piazza and belvedere. The bulk of the offices form two hexagonal courts, both of which allow public access to the building, with the entrance hall placed at the intersection. The council chamber and civic suite are placed on the highest part of the site, to the south, where better views and greater privacy are both possible. One advantage of the hexagonal geometry is that additional wings, if required, can be added.

The building is carried on a grid of concrete columns (either round or hexagonal) but the external walls are built with structured concrete mullions so as to be column-free.

1. Site layout. Key: 1 municipal administrative offices, 2 council chamber and civic suite, 3 future civic halls, 4 civic terrace with car park below, 5 staff car park with service yard below.
2. The model seen from the east.
3. The civic terrace and council chamber, with the administration offices to the right.

4

5

6

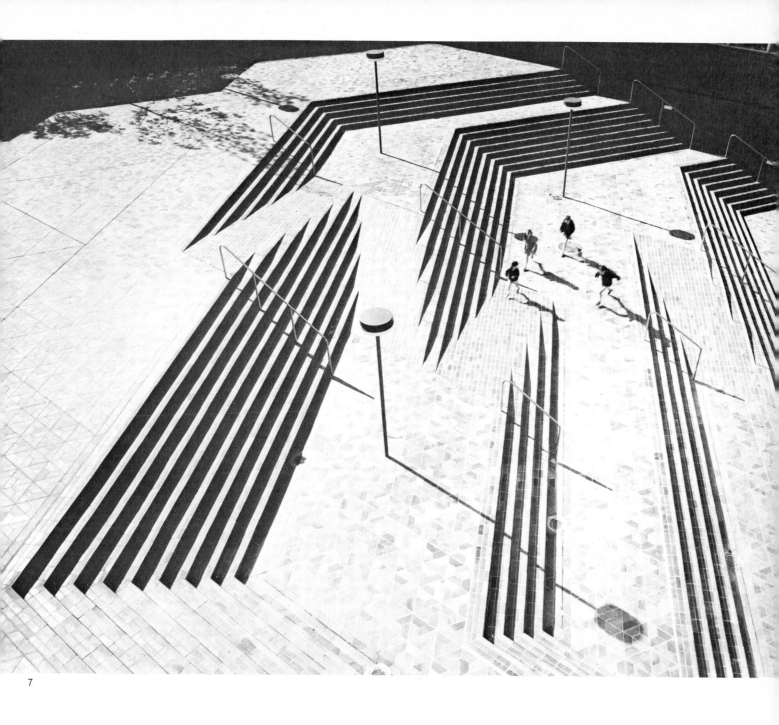

7

4. The steps from the civic terrace to the south court.
5. Service accomodation adds height to the central nucleus containing the main entrance hall.
6. The canteen.
7. Steps and ramps diversify the paving of the north court.

Greater London Council, Department of Architecture and Civic Design
Queen Elizabeth Hall, Purcell Room and Hayward Gallery, South Bank Arts Centre, London, 1963

1. Plans. Key: 1 main entrance, 2 car users' staircase, 3 foyer, 4 bar, 5 cloaks, 6 WC, 7 stage, 8 Queen Elizabeth Hall, 9 Purcell Room artists' room, 10 stage, 11 Purcell Room, 12 terrace, 13 Waterloo Bridge, 14 Hayward Gallery, 15 Royal Festival Hall, 16 terrace.
2. The Hayward Gallery seen from the north-west.

From the time when the Royal Festival Hall was conceived in 1948, it was intended to build a smaller concert hall on the same site. By the time plans for this had matured into a building programme, the brief called for a concert hall to seat 1,100, a recital room to seat 370, and an art gallery to provide a permanent venue for the travelling exhibitions organized by the Arts Council. On a restricted site, overshadowed by the Shell Building, and with a need to preserve some degree of dominance in the role of the Royal Festival Hall, a solution has been found, in planning terms, through the deliberate fragmentation of the complex, using many levels of terrace and walkway to mask the volumes and create an informal and incidental environment.

The two halls and the art gallery are placed orthogonally to each other and to the Waterloo Road boundary to the east. The main foyer, joining the concert hall to the recital room, has been treated in the same asymmetrical manner as the terraces, staircases and service elements; its detachment from the volumes of the auditorium also underlines its interpretation as part of a route system, whether open-air or enclosed. The structure is reinforced concrete throughout, and extremely plastic and sculptural in its handling, creating spaces which are interesting in shape but intimidating in character, so that the illuminated doorways, when we finally locate them, are gratefully approached. Internally, the halls are notable for their elegant furnishings and warm acoustics.

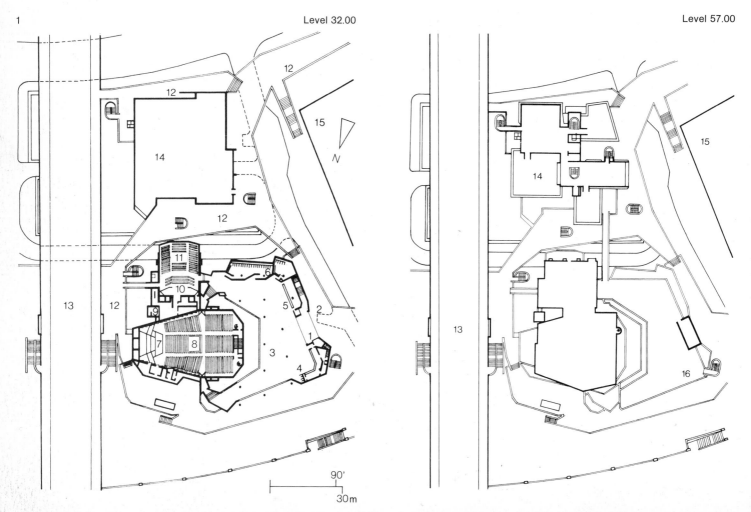

1   Level 32.00   Level 57.00

3, 4. Exhibition rooms in the Hayward Gallery.
5. Queen Elizabeth Hall.
6. Purcell Room.

3

4

5

6

Powell and Moya
Festival Theatre, Chichester, 1961

This theatre was the first professional theatre to be built in England with an 'open' stage. There is no proscenium arch: the audience surrounds the stage on three sides. This layout is justified by a certain school of drama, and has great advantages in terms of building requirements as it does not have to provide an elaborate apparatus of back-stage presentation. Audience and players share the same space, and this has been admirably and neatly expressed by the architects in defining the zones of stage, seating in two tiers, foyer and dressing rooms within the simple volume of a single hexagon. The economy of means, spatially and formally, was dictated by the necessarily limited financial backing for an experimental, if permanent, theatre.

The auditorium is supported on six concrete ribs, one at each corner, but three of them set back into the building to form the cantilevered overhang which shelters the entrance. The roof and the lighting gallery are supported by a hexagonal ring girder in steel tubing, which rests on tension cables bracing the main structure. These can be seen crossing in the centre of the auditorium.

2

1, 2. General views.
3. Plans. Key: 1 main foyer, 2 toilets, 3 coats, 4 dressing room, 5 wardrobe, 6 stage basement, 7 bar store, 8 bar, 9 manager, 10 box office, 11 props, 12 ventilating plant, 13 switch room, 14 stage, 15 stage balcony, 16 backstage, 17 stairs from dressing rooms, 18 stairs from foyer, 19 front gangway, 20 lower tiers, 21 stairs from foyer below, 22 upper tiers, 23 upper gangway, 24 lighting and sound control boxes, 25 gallery.
4. The auditorium. In place of painted arabesques a 'working' ceiling of structure and lighting.

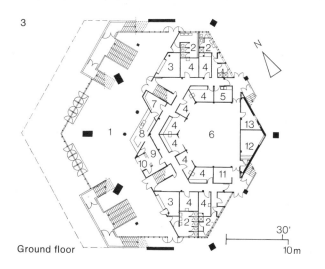

3

Ground floor

30'
10m

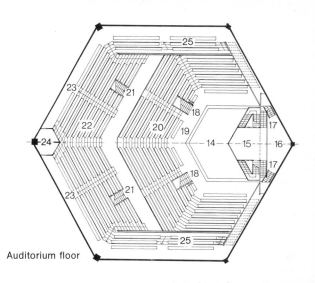

Auditorium floor

4

Peter Moro & Partners
Nottingham Playhouse, 1961

This theatre houses a local repertory company. The theatre policy called for both prosce-nium and open stage productions. This has been achieved with a forestage in two sec-tions, both of which can be adjusted in height up to the level of the main stage. The circular auditorium, 21.3 m. (69 ft. 10 in.) in diameter, defines a clear and intimate space, with seating for more than 700 people. The slatted wall covering is decorative when the lights are on, unobtrusive when the lights are dimmed. Similar slats, again in a circular formation, are used as screening to the overhead forestage lighting concealed in a drum above the stalls. At night the basic geometry of auditorium drum and foyer rectangle is clearly exhibited, so that both internally and externally the functional forms are used as festive decoration.

The structure is a reinforced concrete frame, except for the roofs of the auditorium and stage tower which are steel lattice structures.

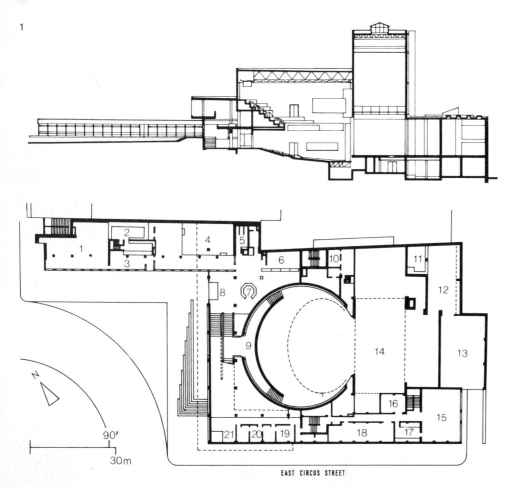

EAST CIRCUS STREET

1. Plan and section. Key: 1 cafeteria, 2 servery, 3 bar, 4 restaurant, 5 WC, 6 cloaks, 7 ticket office, 8 entrance, 9 balcony entrance, 10 venti-lation plant, 11 designers' studio, 12 upper part of paint shop, 13 upper carpenters' shop, 14 upper part of stage, 15 rehearsal room, 16 ward-robe, 17 laundry, 18 wardrobe making, 19 direc-tor, 20 office, 21 lounge.
2. General view from the forecourt, as seen at night.
3. The main foyer.
4. The auditorium.

166

2

3

5

4

Peter Moro & Partners
Gulbenkian Centre, Hull, 1967

This is a drama studio for the study of the theatre under many aspects: it had to be as flexible in layout as possible, with the emphasis on the performance rather than on the spectator. Seating is restricted to about 200, capable of being arranged in banks on one, three or four sides of the stage. The proscenium is created by means of four mobile stage-towers, which are also a part of the elaborate stage lighting system mounted in the ceiling.

The building includes a workshop for the manufacture of scenery, and a generous television studio, as well as the normal ancillaries such as dressing rooms, rehearsal rooms, editing, photographic and graphic studios, etc.

The structure is of concrete, board-marked where exposed, with red brick panels, and a copper roof.

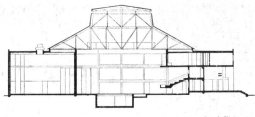

2nd floor

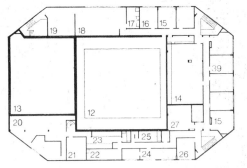

Ground floor

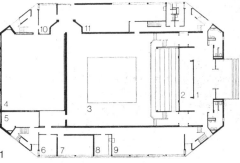

1

2

3

4

1. Plans and section. Key: 1 foyer, 2 cloakrooms, 3 auditorium and stage, 4 TV and film studio, 5 communications centre, 6 control room, 7 sound broadcast studio, 8 dressing room and make-up, 9 TV and repair workshop, 10 model making, 11 workshop and scenery store, 12 upper stage and auditorium, 13 upper TV and film studio, 14 rehearsal room, 15 staff rooms (drama), 16 stage director, 17 laundry, 18 costume making and storage, 19 property store, 20 plant room, 21 animation, 22 graphics, 23 photo studio, 24 editing, 25 darkroom, 26 drama reading and seminar, 27 film preview theatre.
2. General view of the building.
3. The auditorium set up as a proscenium theatre.
4. The auditorium set up as a theatre-in-the-round.

Lord Snowdon, in association with Cedric Price and Frank Newby
Aviary, London Zoological Gardens, 1962

The brief for this aviary, which was intended for a wide range of Indian and African birds, asked for a volume large enough to permit free flight, and for a public viewing route through the space rather than around it. Advantage was taken of the steep slope of the site (adjoining the Regents Canal) to make a garden at two different levels with some variation of flora to accommodate different categories of bird (water, ground-dwelling, cliff-nesting and tree-dwelling). A large volume was created by supporting wire mesh over tension cables, in turn stretched over a series of triangulated frames in tubular aluminium. These frames are themselves carried by wires on shearlegs at either end, thus creating a tensegrity structure in the Buckminster Fuller tradition. The main steel cables are of high tensile steel sheathed in black plastic. The public path takes a zig-zag course through the length of the space, rectangular in plan, crossing the middle as a cantilevered bridge so that birds may be viewed from above as well as from below.

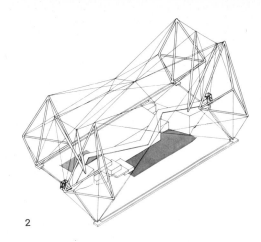

2

1. The west end of the aviary.
2. Axonometric view showing the structure.
3. Plan.
4. The view inside the cage from the lower level.

1

3

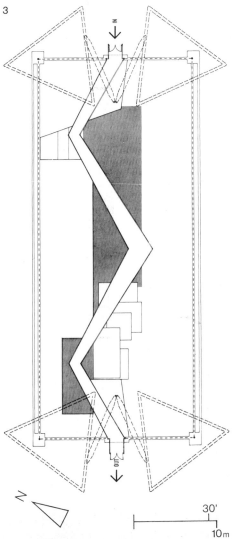

30'

10m

1

Gillespie, Kidd & Coia
St Bride's church and presbytery, East Kilbride, 1960

The building has been conceived as a massive volume isolated from its surroundings and intensively inward in character. The steep site allows it to dominate a considerable area of the town, and adds a touch of the redoubt to the necessarily domestic scale of the adjoining presbytery, which psychologically and architecturally may be said to mediate between the sacred and the secular.

The plan of the church, which seats about 800, is in the form of a broad rectangle, with a free-standing gallery along one side under which are placed a side chapel, confessionals and a baptistry. The nave is a few steps lower than the narthex, defined by this gallery, and especially noteworthy is the way in which this change of levels has been extended to give a special identity to the font.

The structure is of brickwork, with a rough-textured facing skin. The floor is paved in stone, with brick trim, and the ceiling consists of varnished pine slats concealing a steel-framed roof and patent glazing.

1. General view of the church.
2. The presbytery gains drama from the steeply falling site.
3. Plan and section. Key: 1 altar, 2 lady chapel, 3 mortuary chapel, 4 narthex, 5 baptistery, 6 sacristy, 7 tower, 8 plaza, 9 presbytery.
4. The interior of the church.
5. The font is given identity by being placed at the level of the nave, a few steps below the level of the narthex.

1

2

4

3

5

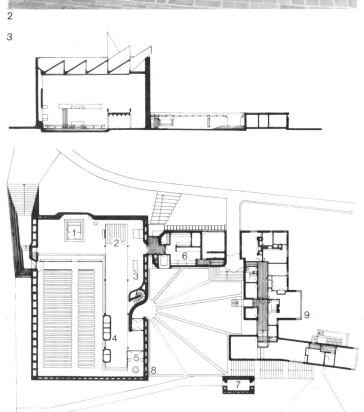

90'

30m

1

Sir Basil Spence, Glover & Ferguson
Mortonhall Crematorium, Edinburgh, 1964

The crematorium is sited in a hollow beside a stream in dense woodland. Access (for cars) is by an extension of the driveway which serves the adjoining cemetery. A waiting shelter lies adjacent to the car park. From here mourners join the cortège and proceed on foot to one of the two chapels. The large chapel faces south and the small one south-west, while the crematorium and services block lie behind at a lower level. A small remembrance chapel is placed separately at some distance to the west.
The concept of the chapels relies on a series of massive walls, angled on plan, and separated by tall and narrow windows with coloured glass. Lanterns above the altars flood this zone with white light.

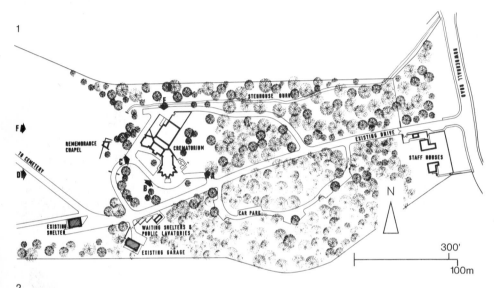

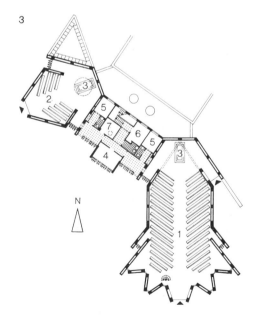

1. Site layout.
2. The entrance front of the main chapel.
3. Plan. Key: 1 main chapel, 2 minor chapel, 3 catafalque, 4 priest, 5 devotion room, 6 staff room, 7 resting room.
4, 5. The interior of the main chapel.
6. General view from the south-west.

4

5

6

Denys Lasdun
Royal College of Physicians, Regents Park, London, 1961

This building is the headquarters for a learned society, concerned with the furtherance of medicine. The important accommodation, consisting of entrance hall, library and dining room as well as executive and conference rooms, forms a ship-like volume, wider above and narrower below, arranged with the narrow end facing the Royal Park. Attached to this volume like appendages are the administration offices, which maintain continuity with the street facades in Albany Street, and the lecture theatre, which is partly submerged below ground level.
The main bulk is faced with white mosaic tiles, and the two dependent volumes are faced in dark brickwork. The white mosaic represents permanence, the dark brickwork transience. The permanent realm is associated with the ceremonial life of the institution; the transient realm with its day-to-day concerns.

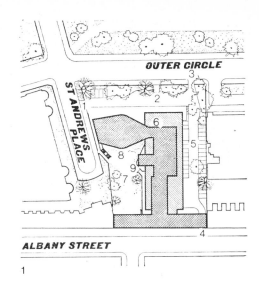

1

2

3

4

1. Site layout. Key: 1 main entrance for vehicles,
2 main entrance for pedestrians, 3 main exit for
vehicles, 4 service entrance, 5 parking area, 6
main entrance to building, 7 garden court, 8 lecture hall, 9 pool.
2, 3. General views of the complex across St
Andrews Place.
4. The service entrance.
5. Plan of the ground floor and section. Key:
1 auditorium, 2 censor's room, 3 council room,
4 large committee room, 5 president's office, 6
registrar's office, 7 treasurer's office, 8 assistant
treasurer's office, 9 secretary's office, 10 assistant
secretary's office, 11 typing pool, 12 accounts
office, 13 working room for post, etc., 14 MRCP
office, 15 entrance hall, 16 main hall, 17 staff rest
room, 18 small lecture room, 19 quiet room, 20
sitting room, 21 upper gallery.
6. The main hall.

5

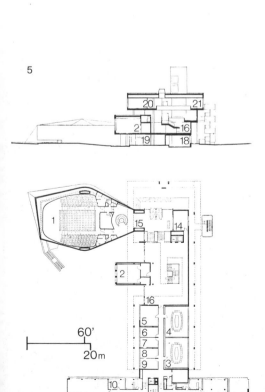

60'
20m

6

5

Gollins Melvin Ward and Partners
Commercial Union Building, London, 1964

The architects were commissioned independently by two rich City firms on adjacent sites. They suggested a comprehensive development in which the original boundaries would be adjusted in order to create a more spacious development with an open piazza in this area of dense narrow streets.

The gain of space allowed two square towers, which gave the most favourable proportion of gross to nett floor space within the daylighting code. The building illustrated here is the higher tower, at 24 storeys above ground, not including the high entrance hall and two storeys accommodating structure and services. The floors and the extension walls are hung from cantilevers carried on a central core. The steel hangers are concealed between alternating mullions of the aluminium curtain wall.

The building provides approximately 26,000 square m. (288,000 square ft.) of office space, with additional staff amenity areas including a restaurant to seat 800 underneath the piazza. The whole floor above the entrance hall is reserved for use as part of a raised walkway system to be developed by the City of London. Spaces for 178 cars are provided in the basement.

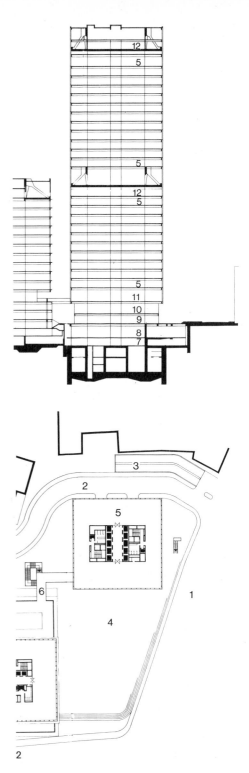

1

1. Looking east across the entrance hall. The lack of clutter is American rather than English in style.
2. Plan of a typical floor and section. Key: 1 St Mary Avenue, 2 minor road, 3 ramp, 4 piazza, 5 typical floor, 6 bridge on podium level, 7 car park, 8 restaurant, 9 hall, 10 mezzanine, 11 podium, 12 plant room.
3. General view.
4. Typical office floor, before occupation. Grey aluminium windows, grey glass, grey vinyl floor, white walls, white louvre drapes on windows. The aggressive ceiling lighting strikes a jarring note.
5. A typical office space.
6. The entrance hall.

Yorke Rosenberg Mardall
Keddies department store extension and office building in Southend, 1961

This building complex contains additional sales areas in the basement, ground and first floors, linked to the existing store and served by escalators. The second and third floors provide parking for 180 cars. Above the car park is an eight-storey office block. The structure is a reinforced concrete frame faced externally with a Swedish white-glazed ceramic tile, a finish which is carried into deep reveals, accentuating the plastic qualities of the volumes rather than the planar quality of the surfaces.
It is worth noting that the sales area enclosed in the first floor by mainly opaque walls is indistinguishable from the two floors of car parking immediately above it.

2

1

1. Detail of the facade. White tiled surfaces are used to emphasize the plastic depth of the facade.
2, 4. General views.
3. Plans. Key: 1 driveway, 2 car lift, 3 store, 4 lobby, 5 lifts, 6 garage, 7 boiler room, 8 office space.

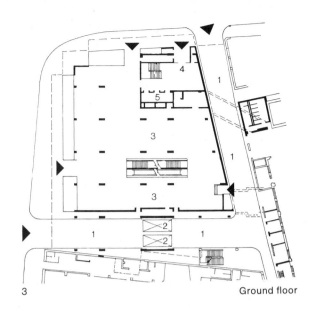

3

Ground floor

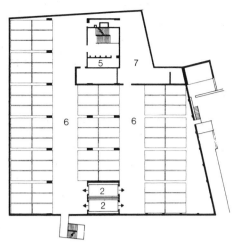

Garage floor

Office floor

4

Yorke Rosenberg Mardall
Factory for Elliott Bros. at Rochester, 1961

This building is a combined facility for design research and the production of electronic equipment and components. Most of the components are very small, although the complete assemblies can be large. The small towers contain the areas for primary production as well as for research; while the heavy work and assembly of large components is confined to the continuous workshop on the ground floor. The towers provide conditions similar to a standard office, except that high standards of lighting and of air-conditioning are required at times for fine work. The assembly areas on the ground floor require conditions equivalent to those for normal light industry. The division of the upper space into separate towers corresponds to the organizational pattern, and the demands of security, while providing a good standard of daylighting. From the main staff entrance hall at one end of the complex a stair leads to a mezzanine corridor along the axis, which gives access to all the various departments. A separate welfare building is projected.

The tower blocks are each carried on a concrete frame with coffered *in situ* concrete floors. The assembly hall has post-stressed concrete T-beams at 3 m. (9 ft. 10 in.) centres spanning 21 m. (68 ft. 11 in.) with continuous cast glass rooflights. All external surfaces are covered in white glazed tiles.

1   Ground floor   Typical upper floor   2

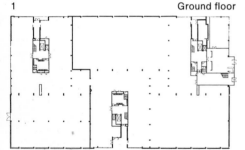
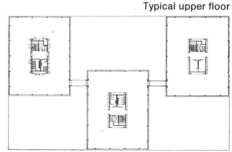

1. Plans.
2. Model.
3. The first three towers, viewed from the side.   18

Alison & Peter Smithson
The Economist group of buildings, St James's, London, 1962

The *Economist* newspaper commissioned the architects' winning design from a limited competition. The planning authority required some residential and commercial accommodation to be provided on the restricted site. Most of the other designs combined these three elements in a single building: the Smithsons gave a separate building to each function, and managed to achieve not only three very compact towers but freed enough space to creat a series of small urban courts between the buildings, on the roof of the podium, which contains mainly parking and services.

The commercial building at the south-west corner contains shops, a banking hall reached by escalators, and a few lettable offices. Its height, limited to four storeys, is in harmony with the frontages to St James's Street. The Economist tower, at the south-east corner, is about twice the height of the adjacent buildings, but this is strangely acceptable in the narrower streets to which it fronts. The third building contains residential accommodation for the nearby Boodles Club and is again adjusted in scale to compare with the old buildings next to it. The end effect of the piazza is quite unlike that of the Commercial Union (pp. 176, 177), but is rather casual and very English. Yet each building is in itself symmetrical and formal, the vertical mullions and the parapets faced with roached Portland stone and the grey enamelled aluminium windows creating an effect of reticence and discretion.

1. The group seen from the side street.
2. Plans. Key: 1 bank entrance hall, 2 shops, 3 tradesmen's entrance, 4 garage ramp to second basement, 5 mail room, 6 multi-copying, 7 canteen, 8 kitchen, 9 cafeteria, 10 stores, 11 dining room, 12 kitchen, 13 steward, 14 staff dining room, 15 kiosk, 16 staff entrance, 17 porter's room, 18 air-conditioning plant, 19 Boodle's Club, 20 bank, 21 Economist offices, 22 residential building, 23 general office area, 24 reception, 25 reception room, 26 reading room, 27 secretary, 28 dining room, 29 bedroom, 30 caretaker's flat.

Piazza floor

Typical upper floor

Ground floor

1st floor above piazza

3

4

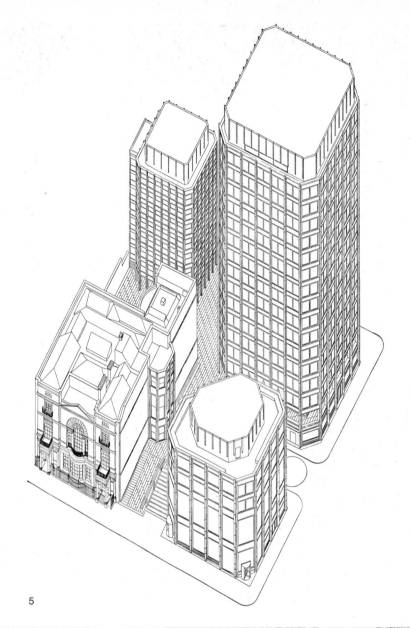

5

6

7

3

3. A view along Bury Street with the residential building and office tower on the right.
4. The piazza looking towards the bank building.
5. Axonometric view.
6. The piazza with office tower (on the left) and residential building (on the right).
7. The hall of the bank building seen from the office tower.

1

Ryder and Yates and Partners
Headquarters for the Northern Gas Board, Killingworth, 1964

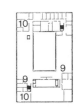

Killingworth is a new township a few miles north of Newcastle-upon-Tyne. The building complex stands in new parkland, beside an artificial lake and the new town centre, in an area which only a few years ago was a scene of industrial wasteland and desolation. As there is plenty of space, the office building is limited to three storeys in height, two floors of regular office accommodation being constructed above a 'free' ground plan. The fenestration of the two upper storeys is specially designed to emphasize the proportion of the enclosed volume: the aluminium frames are two storeys high, with infill panels of vitreous enamelled steel trays which replace horizontal glazing bars, and which mask the service space enclosed between ceiling and structural slab. This space also contains the deep castellated steel beams, which enable the columns in the ground floor to be widely spaced at 6.4 m. (21 ft.), so that the volume of the enclosed offices rides on recessed pilotis in the Corbusian style.

The offices surround and enclose a rectangular courtyard, eccentrically placed in the overall volume, the deeper side containing the entrance hall and a small auditorium.

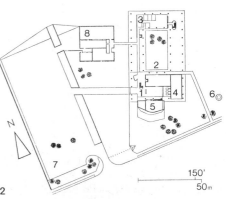

2

150'
50 m

1

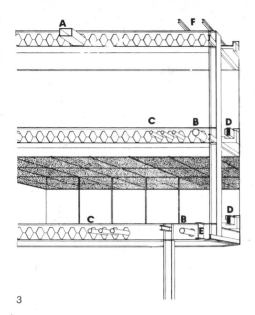

3

4

5

Renton Howard Wood Associates
St Katharine Dock House, London, 1965

This building for the Port of London Authority replaces a block of offices destroyed during the war and houses the Authority's computer and its attendant offices, and a part of its police force administration. Club and canteen facilities are also provided. The site adjoins St Katharine Dock, no longer in commercial use; the old brick warehouses are of an unusually regular and uncompromising character, rising on strong Doric pilotis of cast iron. The decision was made to conform to the lines of the old buildings, which seemed likely to be preserved whatever future was decided for the dock itself. The architects aimed to match their strength and dignity by a bold use of hard-wearing materials. The superstructure is faced with strongly modelled precast concrete units with a crushed-flint aggregate, and is carried on facetted concrete columns.

Offices are contained in the top two floors where peripheral windows are supplemented by two internal courts. The next floor below contains the large canteen and is treated as a piano nobile, with larger scale units in the elevation.

2

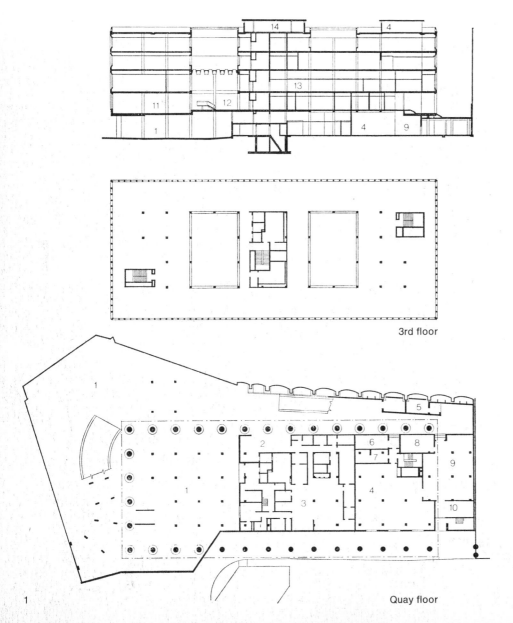

3rd floor

Quay floor

1

1. Plans and section. Key: 1 car park, 2 unloading bay, 3 kitchen, 4 plant room, 5 sub station, 6 switch room, 7 battery room, 8 oil tanks, 9 boiler room, 10 cooling tower, 11 concourse, 12 foyer, 13 canteen servery, 14 penthouse.
2. The design carries on the lines of the existing warehouses.
3. The south face of the building.

Foster Associates
Air Structure for Computer Technology Ltd., Hemel Hempstead, 1970

The client was faced with a rate of expansion which threatened to outstrip the fastest of crash building programmes. At the time the architects were approached, an additional area of some 750 square m. (8,073 square ft.) of office space was urgently required to accommodate 70 people engaged in computer programming and product design. The architects, after investigation, decided that the problem could only be met by an air structure, although such enclosures had not previously been considered feasible for activities more demanding than warehousing and sports halls.

The environmental problems of a thin-wall structure were resolved by a number of technical and planning innovations. These enabled a fully carpeted and serviced office to be realized for a cost of less than £ 1 per square foot. The erection time was 55 minutes. The nylon reinforced PVC enclosure was fabricated in Sweden to the architects' designs. The construction of a future car park on the site was advanced to provide a base for the air structure, which was linked to the existing facility by a combined air-lock and lobby. A multi-purpose thermostatically controlled system combined heating, ventilation and inflation, with standby battery operation. The internal lamp standards provided background light but would have supported the fabric in the event of total deflation. The facility was dismantled after it had served its purpose.

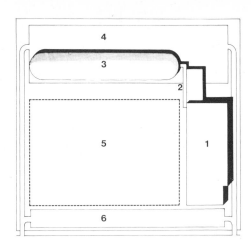

1

2

3

4

5

1, Site layout. Key: 1 existing building, 2 covered link, 3 air structure, 4 car park, 5 new research and development facility, 6 visitors' car park.
2. Plan.
3. At night the rhythm of the fluorescent lighting enlivens the bland volume of the translucent skin.
4. The translucent skin diffuses all light, both natural and artificial.
5. Without its supporting air pressure, the architecture is a mere mass of wrinkles.

1

Foster Associates
Passenger terminal and operations centre for the Olsen Shipping Line, London, 1970

By adopting a linear form the design adapts to the limited space available while showing economies of both construction and operation. Speed of construction was also important, and this influenced the decision to use metal construction, off-site fabrication and dry assembly.

The operations and amenity centres each occupy one floor in a two-storey steel shed which was designed for quick erection while details of the internal arrangements were still being worked out. A long-span steel structure using castellated beams provides an obstruction-free interior capable of flexible rearrangement, and the deep beams allow servicing systems to be inserted as required. The deep space is laid out on office-landscape lines, with a continuous lighting provision in the ceiling. The total glazing, at either end, is in mirrored glass which allows a full view of the outside while affording privacy to the occupants.

The passenger building is elevated to the level of deck access, the necessary ramps being disposed in the dead space between the transit sheds: this leaves the quayside free for the deployment of mechanical equipment. The metal deck floor is carried on steel columns and the enclosure is of plastic-coated steel sheets formed to a self-stiffening profile. Translucent panels admit daylight along the length and humanize the interior without compromising the industrial character.

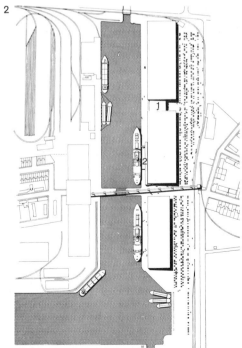

2

1. The operations and amenity building seen from the quayside. Internal activities are screened by the use of mirrored glass.
2. Site plan. Key: 1 operations and amenity building, 2 passenger terminal.
3. The operations and amenity building under construction.
4. Perspective section through the operations and amenity building. The long-span steel structure provides column-free space and a flexible servicing layer.

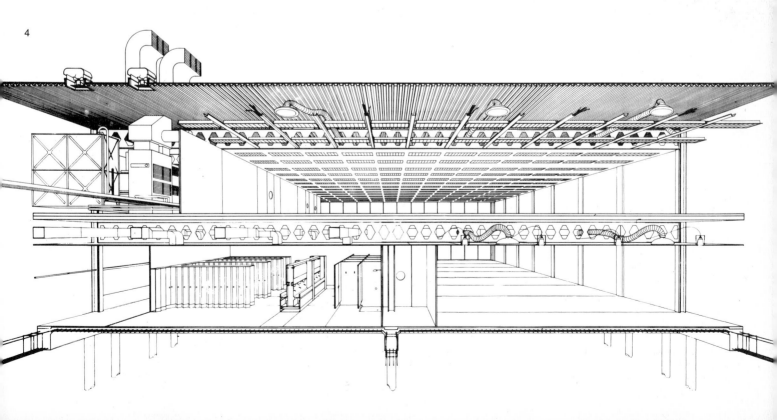

5

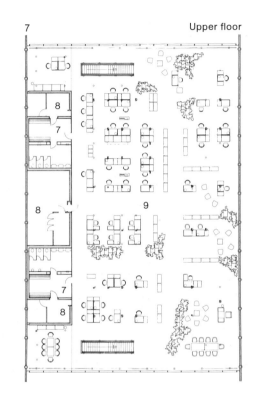

7   Upper floor

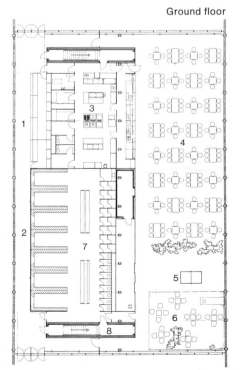

Ground floor

6

1

8

9

5. The operations area is laid out on the office landscape principle.

6. The amenity centre is protected from noise and weather, but has an open view of quayside activities.

7. Plans. Key: 1 reception counter, 2 passage, 3 kitchen, 4 dining room, 5 table tennis, 6 lounge, 7 locker room, 8 plant room, 9 office.

8. The passenger terminal is raised to the level of the ship's gangway, leaving the quayside clear for other activities.

9. A tube is a tube – but the mechanical analogy is humanized by the rhythm of translucent panels.

Bicknell and Hamilton
Telephone exchange and signal box in Birmingham, 1963

This facility houses the equipment and telecommunications necessary for controlling a large sector of railway line following a programme of electrification and modernization. Situated near New Street Station, it is unusual in the size and complexity of its requirements, which include the accommodation of a power signal box controlling some 350 signals and 500 track circuits, a telephone exchange, teleprinters, a pneumatic tube system and specialist workshops, stores and ancillary areas. The building comprises five levels, only the top one of which has the traditional functions of a signal box. The structure is of reinforced concrete, with pre-stressed floor units capable of withstanding heavy loads. The penthouse containing the signal control room has an uncased steel frame and a timber roof. The external cladding units are of precast concrete with a heavily serrated profile of exposed aggregate. The projecting roof provides glare-free lighting of the control console – not a shaded view of the tracks!

1

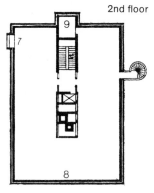

3rd floor

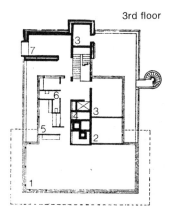

2nd floor

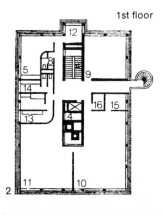

1st floor

2

3

1. The box seen across the railway tracks.
2. Plans. Key: 1 console room, 2 indicator room, 3 plant room, 4 ducts, 5 mess room, 6 men's WC, 7 service entrance, 8 relay room, 9 battery room, 10 telegraph office, 11 manual exchange, 12 men's locker room, 13 women's locker room, 14 women's WC, 15 clerk, 16 store.
4. The street elevation of the building.

Bicknell and Hamilton
Maintenance depot for British Rail at Paddington Station, London, 1965

This group of buildings contains maintenance workshops for vehicles and plant, and warehousing. The site is bounded on all sides by movement systems, the most hectic of which is the elevated M4 motorway and the most peaceful the still-used Regents Canal. The site extends under the elevated road and this section has the warehouse. The east block contains vehicle maintenance facilities and is designed as a top-lit flexible working area. The west block, which rises through four storeys, contains maintenance workshops, a paint shop and boiler room at ground level, technical stores at first floor level, light workshops at second floor level, and staff rooms and offices on the top floor.

As the building had to adapt in form to a very restricted site, it is constructed of *in situ* concrete; only the roof of the vehicle depot has repeating precast units. The proximity of the motorway, as well as the functions, dictated a heavy form of construction which is unusually resistant to fire and noise.

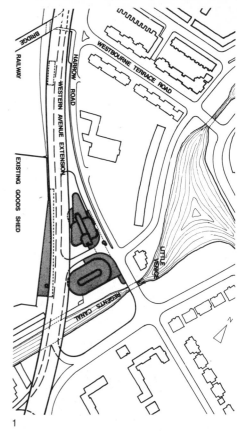

1

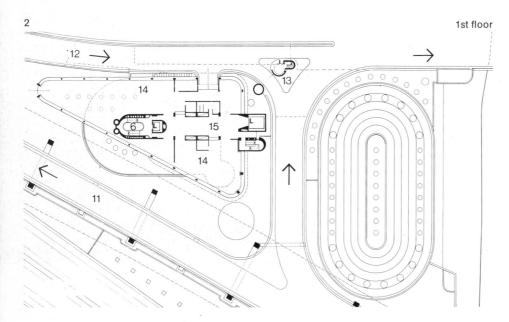

1st floor

Ground floor

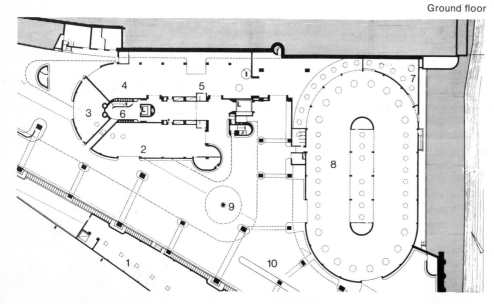

1. Site layout.
2. Plans. Key: 1 warehouse, 2 paint shop, 3 boilers, 4 heavy plant, 5 carpentry shop, 6 stairs, 7 sheet metal shop, 8 vehicle servicing, 9 steam wash, 10 fuelling point, 11 Harrow Road, 12 ramp, 13 gate house, 14 stores, 15 hall.
3. The west block seen from the lowest road level, with the double-deck elevated motorway on the right and access ramp on the left.
4. Section through the west block.

19

3

4

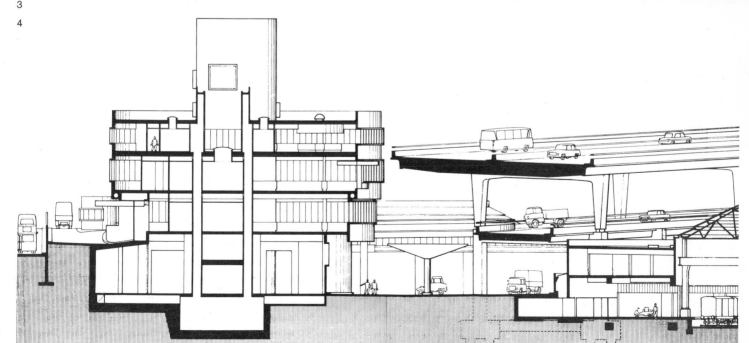

7

5. The roof of the vehicle servicing hall.
6. The total complex seen from the east, with the Regents Canal in the foreground.

5

6

1

Index

Aalto, Alvar 26
Abercrombie, Patrick 9
Architects' Co-Partnership 94
Aslin, C. H. 9, 19
Arup, Ove 94
Arup Associates 25, 80, 110
Attenborough + Jones 88, 146

Banham, Reyner 10, 20, 31
Barthes, Roland 20, 31
Bernini, Gianlorenzo 18
Bicknell and Hamilton 194, 196
Brawne, Michael 25, 44
Brett, Lionel 8, 9, 31, 48
Brett and Pollen 48

Cadbury-Brown, H. T., and Partners 152
Cassirer, Ernst 14, 31
Casson, Hugh 9
Castle Park Dean Hook 104
Chamberlin, Powell & Bon 23, 65
Chalk, Warren 31
Churchill, Sir Winston 9
Colquhoun, Alan 31
Cullen, Gordon 9
Cullinan, Edward 29, 30

Dannatt, Trevor 25, 26
Dean, Christopher 31
Derbyshire, Andrew 19

Elgar, Sir Edward 12
Erskine, Ralph 92

Farrell/Grimshaw Partnership 29, 68
Farrell, Terence 29
Foster, Norman 29, 52
Foster, W. 52
Foster Associates 188, 190
Fourier, Jean Baptiste Joseph 20
Frampton, Kenneth 14, 31

Gasson, Barry 42
Gillespie Kidd & Coia 84, 170
Gollins Melvin Ward and Partners 176
Gowan, James 16, 19, 24, 31, 34, 116
Greater London Council 9, 72, 74, 140, 142,
    158
Grimshaw, Nicolas 29
Gropius, Walter 16

Herron, Ron 31
Herzberg 31
Hitler, Adolf 28
Hodgkinson, Patrick 70, 102
Howard, Ebenezer 9
Howell, Killick, Partridge and Amis 24, 72, 78, 90,
    144
Howell, William 31
Huxtable, Ada Louise 31

James, Lord 19
Jameson, Conrad 31
Jenkins, Frank 31
Joedicke, Jürgen 31
Johnson, Philip 9, 17, 21

Kallmann, McKinnell and Knowles 25
Kaufmann, Emil 31
Killick, John 31

Laird, Michael, and Partners 131
Lanham, Douglas 102
Lasdun, Denys 27, 28
Lasdun, Denys, & Partners 28, 128

Le Corbusier 10, 11, 13, 14, 17, 20, 21, 25, 27, 28,
    29, 31, 184
Ledoux, Claude-Nicolas 20
Llewelyn-Davies Weeks Forestier-Walker & Bor
    25, 132
Long, Mary Jane 40
Lubetkin, Berthold 8, 31
Lutyens, Sir Edwin 12, 18
Lyons Israel Ellis Partnership 112

Magritte, René 28
Marlborough, Sara Duchess of 18
Martin, Sir Leslie 19, 70, 82, 102
Matthew, Robert 19
Matthew, Robert, Johnson-Marshall & Partners
    19, 126, 150
Maxwell, Robert 31
Mercury Housing Society Ltd 68
Meunier, John 42
Meyer, Hannes 13, 14, 15, 16, 18, 20, 21, 22, 23,
    27, 29, 31
Mies van der Rohe, Ludwig 10, 13, 14, 15, 21, 25
Moretti 10
Moro, Peter, & Partners 164, 166
Myerson, Martin 31

Nairn, Ian 9
Nash, John 20
Newby, Frank 168
Neylan and Ungless 60, 62
Niemeyer, Oscar 10

Ozenfant, Amédée 31

Palladio, Andrea 11, 31
Panofsky, Erwin 27, 31
Paolozzi, Eduardo 39
Parkes 19
Paxton, Sir Joseph 9
Peacock, Thomas Love 25
Pevsner, Nikolaus 8, 9, 10, 12
Phippen/Randall and Parkes 54, 57
Powell and Moya 22, 23, 86, 162
Price, Cedric 7, 23, 29, 168

Renton Howard Wood Associates 107, 186
Richards, Brian 152
Rogers, Richard + Su 29, 50, 52
Rowe, Colin 31
Rudolph, Paul 21
Ryder and Yates and Partners 184

Saussure, Horace Bénédict de 31
Schnaidt, Claude 13, 16, 31
Scott, Sir George Gilbert 100
Seifert, Richard 9, 22, 23
Sheppard, Richard, Robson & Partners 24, 124
Skidmore, Owings & Merrill (SOM) 21, 28
Smithson, Alison & Peter 10, 11, 12, 15, 19, 20,
    21, 28, 31, 181
Snowdon, Lord 168
Spence, Sir Basil 9, 24, 25, 27
Spence, Sir Basil, Bonnington & Collins 25, 28
    122, 155
Spence, Sir Basil, Glover & Ferguson 172
Stalin, Joseph Vissarionovich 16
Stillman and Eastwick-Field 26, 27, 138
Stirling, James 17, 19, 24, 28, 96, 98, 116,
    119
Stout & Litchfield 46

Team 10 21
Tiege, K. 31

Vanbrugh, Sir John 18
Venturi, Robert 21, 27, 31
Voelcker, John 31
Voysey, Charles F. Annesley 11

Weeks, John 17
Whitfield, William 100
Wilford, Michael 119
Wilson, Colin St John 38, 40, 82, 102
Wilson, Sandy 31
Winter, John and Associates 32
Womersley, J. L. 19
Womersley, Peter 135, 148
Wren, Sir Christopher 18
Wright, Frank Lloyd 13, 18, 29

Yorke Rosenberg Mardall 22, 28, 29, 178, 180

Photographers' Credits

Behr Photography, London 25 (19), 44 (1), 45 (3, 5, 6), 175 (3)

Brecht-Einzig Ltd., London 22 (11), 29 (29), 39 (5, 6), 46 (1), 47 (3, 4), 51 (6), 52 (2), 53 (5), 61 (4), 78 (1), 91 (4), 96 (2), 97 (3), 98 (1), 113 (2-4), 114 (5), 115 (6-8), 117 (3), 119 (1), 120 (2), 121 (5-7), 128 (1), 152 (2), 154 (4), 174 (2), 175 (6), 193 (9), 197 (3), 198 (6)

Studio Brett, Glasgow 85 (3)

Lewis Brown Associates, Birmingham 194 (1), 195 (3)

H. de Burgh Galwey, London 23 (13, 14), 94 (2), 100 (1, 2), 139 (3)

Camera Craft, Truro 51 (7)

Michael Carapetian, London 11 (6), 182 (3, 4, 6), 183 (7)

Castle Park Dean Hook, London 101 (3, 4)

Frank Donaldson 26 (21)

John Donat, London 33 (2, 3, 4), 35 (4), 36 (6), 80 (1, 2), 81 (4), 83 (3, 4, 6), 94 (1), 95 (4, 5), 99 (3), 102 (2), 103 (3), 110 (1, 2), 111 (5), 116 (1), 118 (4, 5), 130 (2), 144 (1), 145 (3, 4), 165 (3), 189 (5)

Keith Gibson, Keighley 126 (1), 127 (2, 4), 150 (1), 151 (3, 4)

James Gowan, London 34 (2), 37 (9, 10)

Greater London Council 74 (1, 2), 75 (4), 76 (6), 77 (7), 141 (3, 4), 142 (1), 143 (2, 6, 7), 159 (2), 160 (3), 161 (5, 6)

Bruno de Hamel, London 90 (2), 91 (5)

Archie Hanford Ltd., Croydon 29 (27)

A. L. Hunter, Edinburgh 173 (5, 6)

Allan Hurst, Nottingham 165 (2, 4)

A. F. Kersting, London 40 (2), 41 (5)

Robert Kirkman 28 (26)

Sam Lambert, London 24 (15, 16), 55 (3, 4), 56 (5, 6), 57 (1), 58 (5), 59 (7, 8, 9), 60 (1), 61 (5), 65 (2), 66 (3, 4), 67 (8), 136 (3, 4), 137 (5-7), 168 (1), 169 (4), 171 (5)

Denys Lasdun, London 175 (4)

John Maltby Ltd., London 66 (5, 6), 67 (9)

Mann Brothers, London 70 (2)

Eric de Maré, London 48 (1), 49 (3, 4), 90 (1)

Photo Mayo Ltd., Newcastle upon Tyne 185 (4, 5)

Sydney W. Newbery, London 79 (4, 5, 6)

Ian A. Niamath, London 128 (2), 129 (4)

Park Studios, Hatfield 54 (1)

Philipson Studios, Newcastle upon Tyne 184 (1)

John Rawson, London 22 (12), 41 (4)

John Rose + John Dyble, Kenton 177 (4)

Henk Snoek Photography & Associates, London 25 (18, 20), 27 (23), 26 (22), 38 (2), 39 (4), 42 (1), 43 (4, 5), 72 (1), 73 (3), 89 (2, 3, 4), 107 (1), 108 (3-5), 109 (6), 122 (2), 123 (3, 6, 7), 124 (1), 125 (3-5), 130 (3), 131 (6), 133 (3-5), 134 (7), 135 (1), 155 (2, 3), 156 (5, 6), 157 (7), 172 (2), 173 (4), 176 (1), 177 (3, 5, 6), 178 (1, 2), 180 (2, 3), 181 (1), 186 (2), 187 (3)

Stillman and Eastwick-Field, London 139 (4, 5)

Ezra Stoller, New York 21 (9, 10), 51 (4)

Tim Street-Porter, London 92 (1), 93 (3-5), 192 (6), 198 (5)

Bill Toomey 10 (5)

Wm. J. Toomey 10 (3), 56 (8), 163 (4), 172 (1, 2)

Gerhard Ullmann, Berlin 19 (8)

Waverley Studios, Galashiels 149 (2-4)

Colin Westwood, London 24 (17), 146 (1), 147 (3-5), 166 (2), 167 (3, 4)

Ralph Williamson, Enfield 179 (4)

G. Forrest Wilson, Glasgow 170 (1), 172 (2)